*Meditations From The Minstrel
12 Months of Meditations For Your
Mind, Body and Spirit*

*By. Pastor Jacqueline
Faye Saunders-Johnson*

Meditations From The Minstrel

Compiled by B. C. CaBell

All scripture references are from the King James Version of the Holy Bible unless otherwise specified.

Introduction

The Miriam-Webster Dictionary describes the word meditate as;

Intransitive verb

: to engage in contemplation or reflection

: to engage in mental exercise (as concentration on one's breathing or repetition of a mantra) for the purpose of reaching a heightened level of spiritual awareness

Transitive verb

: to focus one's thoughts on : reflect on or ponder over

: to plan or project in the mind : intend, purpose

In this devotional Pastor Jacqueline Faye Saunders-Johnson gives the children of God a tool for the total and continued healing of the Body of Christ. This devotional and study guide gives readers a structure we so desperately need – a composition for true study of the promises of God.

So often we grab our devotionals, read a scripture, a short story, a one minute prayer and go on about our day without the promises of what we have read ever really taking root in our spirit. This work is very different. Pastor Johnson has taken her time to choose not daily, but monthly scripture lessons to give the reader the opportunity to meditate on and become one with the Word of God.

Each month is a carefully selected passage of scripture along with questions, comments, truths, and revelations in order to give every reader a firm foundation and deeper understanding of what he or she has read. Pastor Jackie Johnson is seeking to feed the people of God with food that will sustain.

The Lord's Prayer, a powerful and significant prayer tool in the arsenal of Christians, chastens us to seek from the Lord "…this day our daily bread." We are to pray daily for the bread that will satiate us. The Holy Bible does not implore us to ask for our weekly, monthly, or yearly bread but our daily bread. We are to "die daily". *Meditations From The Minstrel* is a potent work to help God's people seek, find, and be blessed with daily word for daily living.

Pastor Jacqueline Faye Saunders-Johnson

Pastor Jackie Johnson is one of the most prolific women of God given to this generation. She is a powerfully anointed woman not only in the pulpit but also behind the keyboard. Pastor Johnson is a world-renowned musician with a connection so great with the Holy Spirit that she is known as a minstrel. You can read more about the woman of God in the back of this devotional.

Acknowledgements

After much prayer and a leap of faith, this work has come to be put in this form to share with the people of the body of Christ. First, I want to give thanks to the two people that have helped to shape and mold my life. The late great Chief Apostle, Dr. Monroe R. Saunders, Sr., who is my DAD, instilled in me all of the attributes that I carry in my ministry today. He taught me that the POWER IS IN THE LOVE, and that DELIVERANCE IS IN MY PRAISE. He is with me whenever I minister and flow in the Spirit.

Then my mother, Elect Lady Alberta Saunders instilled in me all the attributes of being a lady, a wife, a mother, and grandmother. She is one that I can share with and get advice from. She also gave me the inspiration as the founder of the Abundant Life Retreat Ministry with her beloved husband, Dr. Monroe R. Saunders, Sr. which all of this has flowed from.

I would also like to thank my husband, Dr. Robert E. Johnson, Sr., who has been my inspiration and support to become who and what I am today. He has been my backbone and support and has pushed me into this ministry where women are sometimes frowned upon. So I thank him from the bottom of my heart for his support and love.

I thank my children and church family, New Jerusalem Praise Tabernacle, who also have supported me in my every endeavor. And finally, I thank Briana CaBell who has labored to put this work together. She has a definite skill and ability and was determined to put my heart and thoughts on paper. This has been a monumental task that she has undertaken and accomplished to have this finished work in your hand. Special thanks to Briana's mother, Mrs. Cynthia Williams, who served as the proof-reader for the project. I thank God for the gift and talent that He has bestowed upon each of you and most of all, I thank you for your love and faith in me to be your shepherd.

I pray that these devotions are as much a blessing for you to read and hold onto as it has been for me to produce it. GOD BLESS AND KEEP YOU!

-Pastor Jacqueline Faye Saunders-Johnson

January

The Everlasting Promise

There shall not any man be able to stand before thee all the days of thy life: as I was with Moses, so I will be with thee: I will not fail thee, nor forsake thee.

Joshua 1:5

A key element in the life of modern day Christians is the spiritual warfare we face day after day. Remembering that, "there is nothing new under the sun", we can understand that warfare is not new but in this generation we face a unique set of challenges. The wicked prosper greatly, the ways of the world are all around us, sin and ungodliness are prominent, accepted and even encouraged, and many of our brethren are sick, dying, and victims of all sorts of hurt and pain. With these things weighing on us how can we be confident that the Lord is still with us and will not fail nor forsake us? Let's look at the circumstances surrounding this verse.

This commission given to Joshua comes after the death of Moses (vss. 1-2). The fact that this came after Moses' death is quite significant because the continuation of God's purposes to move Israel into the land, for certain typological reasons, could only come only after his death. Why is this?

Moses was the great lawgiver who represented the Law of Sinai, which demonstrates the perfect holiness of God and the sinful state of man who stands separated from God (Rom. 3:23). But the Law, though holy, good and perfect, could neither give life, spirituality nor justification.

Moses portrayed the law, which cannot lead us into the saving and abundant life of Christ. It was merely a guide, a temporary set of rules for the time, it could not take away sin or provide deliverance from the flesh. Why? Because it was weak in that it was dependent upon man and his ability (Rom. 8:3-4). The Law provided a righteous standard, but no power or grace for the flesh or indwelling sin (Rom. 6:14; 8:3f).

Because of this, Moses had to pass on before Joshua could be commissioned and given orders to take the people across Jordan and into the Promised Land. A further reason is seen in Joshua's name which so clearly reminds us that "*Yahweh* is Salvation." As the Hebrew equivalent of Jesus, Joshua typifies the Lord Jesus and His saving life who provides us not only with redemption, but with the power we need to enter into the possession of our possessions in Christ.

With the mention of the death of Moses, Joshua is then told, "Now therefore arise, cross this Jordan, you and all this people." By way of application for today, the words "**Now therefore arise**," (in view of the death of Moses and what he represented) teach us the truth that no man can live the Christian life by keeping a set of laws or taboos. While the Christian life involves obedience to the principles and imperatives of the Word, it is more. It is a life to be lived by faith in the power of God. We simply cannot live the Christian life in our own energy or by our own determination. The Christian life is not just being Mr. Nice or merely keeping a set of Christian principles and rules. It is a faith relationship with God to be lived out in the power of the Spirit and in the light of the Word.

With the Words, **"arise, cross this Jordan,"** the Lord is saying, "get out of the desert and move on into Canaan." God's will for the believer is never in the wilderness. It is in Canaan, the place of deliverance and conquest. "Arise, cross" by the parallel of New Testament truth says, "take up your armor, use your supernatural resources, stop trusting in yourself, trust me and move out."

"You and all this people" illustrates that spirituality is not just for an elect few, but it is for all believers. The abundant, maturing Christian life is God's plan and will for every single believer. It is only limited by our lack of availability to His constant availability to us. Every believer is blessed with every spiritual blessing, is a priest of God with abundant grace available for every situation. We need to remember all Israel got out of Egypt the same way—by faith in God's grace, and they would all cross over Jordan in exactly the same way, by faith in God's deliverance.

The words, **"to the land which I am giving you"** and in verse 3, **"every place on which ..."** illustrates the truth of Ephesians 1:3 and Colossians 2:10. "I am giving you" and "I have given it to you" shows us God was then in the process of bringing to pass that which had been theirs all along. Joshua 2:9-11 reveals that the land had virtually been theirs for 40 years. It was just waiting to be possessed. And like that, from the moment of salvation, God has provided every believer with every spiritual blessing and provision. Of course, as this book makes perfectly clear, having title deed to the land (or our blessings in Christ) does not mean our lives will be without testing, conflict, struggles, and pressures. It indeed will, but since the battle is the Lord's, since God has done the most for us in Christ, with the testings and temptations comes God's deliverance through faith and the application of the Word.

In verse 5, Joshua is given the promise, **"no man will be able to stand before you,"** but this promise is also a warning. While the land was theirs for the taking, it would not be taken without conflict or battle. And likewise, as the land of Canaan was full of fortified cities and enemies that needed to be driven out, so the Christian life is a life of conflict with enemies which must be overcome. Though the outcome is assured if we claim God's sufficiency and the saving life of Christ, we must still do battle and reckon with the fact of the enemy throughout this life. This is a wakeup call, a reality that must be faced: life is full of battles and conflicts. I don't know about you but I live in Maryland, not in Eden, nor are we in the millennial reign of Christ. Rather we wrestle with the flesh (indwelling sin), with the devil and supernatural powers of darkness, and a world system that is antagonistic to God, to His Word, and to godly living (cf. Rom. 7:15f; Gal. 5:16f; Eph. 5:15-16; 6:10f; 1 Pet. 5:8-9).

Nevertheless, the positive side is that these words, "no man will be able to stand before you ..." are also a promise of continued deliverance in battle after battle after battle. Because of the infinite sufficiency of the saving life of the Christ through His finished work on the cross, His triumphant presence at the right hand of God, our identification with Him in His death, resurrection and session in heaven, and through His gift of the Holy Spirit, there is no enemy we can possibly face which the Lord (our Joshua) has not already conquered. Our need is to appropriate what He has already done for us through the wise faith-application of His Word.

Though still active and roaming about, Satan's power has been broken and we can resist his deceptions and attacks. Though the sin principle still dwells within or the flesh is still active in our members, its power over us has been broken through our union with Christ in His death and resurrection. This means the victory of possessing our possessions is through the gift of the

Holy Spirit (Rom. 6 and 8) and the sanctifying power of a Word-filled life.

We all entertain the desire to live in an ideal world, where life moves along smoothly without problems or stress. In fact, we were created for such and it is not wrong to long for that time which will come with the return of the Lord Jesus, our Joshua. But the doctrines of the apostasy of the last days, the evil nature of this day and time, plus the presence of our three enemies are constant reminders that such cannot be the case now any more than we can have lasting and true world peace without the return of the Lord. We must face the facts and be prepared to face life as it really is. In Christ we are super-conquerors and through His saving life we can overcome the individual battles of life, but we must be prepared to fight the good fight.

We all like to rock along without anything upsetting our schedules or forcing us out of our comfort zones. When we attempt to get away from the struggle, God jars us back into reality through some unpleasant condition or experience and we are again faced with reality. After vacation we must go back to work and face that co-worker who is so hard to get along with. We are going along and then suddenly, there is a threat to our health or that of our spouse or child. Or we may face the death of a loved one which brings heartache, loneliness, along with new pressures and responsibilities. Such is your life and mine, but the words "no man will be able to stand before you all the days of your life" intrudes into our lives with two realities: a warning and promise.

The words, **"just as I have been with Moses, I will be with you; I will not fail you or forsake you,"** call our attention to one of the great truths of the Bible. Israel would get into the land the *same way* they got out of Egypt. Likewise, we enter into the abundant life of Christ the *same way* we were delivered from wrath—by faith in the saving life of Christ. Just as we trusted in Christ and the accomplishments of the cross for justification and redemption, so we must reckon on those same accomplishments as the basis for our security and daily deliverance (Rom. 6:4-11; Col. 2:6-3:3).

Questions To Ask Myself This Month

1. God promised Joshua that he would neither fail nor forsake him. What has He promised you? Have those promises come to fruition?

_____

_____

_____

_____

2. Consider the ministry calling that God gave to Joshua. What leadership role has the Lord called you to? How have/will you answer?

_____

_____

_____

_____

3. What has or may be tempting you to disobey the appointment of God?

_____

_____

_____

_____

4. The passing of Moses and the appointment of Joshua can symbolize the end of an old era, mindset, or position, and the beginning of a new one. Have you experienced your time of coming into a new area? What were the situations surrounding it? (See 2 Corinthians 5:17)

_____

_____

_____

_____

Additional Notes

February

Real Love

Though I speak with the tongues of men and of angels, and have not charity, I am become as sounding brass, or a tinkling cymbal.

And though I have the gift of prophecy, and understand all mysteries, and all knowledge; and though I have all faith, so that I could remove mountains, and have not charity, I am nothing.

And though I bestow all my goods to feed the poor, and though I give my body to be burned, and have not charity, it profiteth me nothing.

Charity suffereth long, and is kind; charity envieth not; charity vaunteth not itself, is not puffed up,

Doth not behave itself unseemly, seeketh not her own, is not easily provoked, thinketh no evil;

Rejoiceth not in iniquity, but rejoiceth in the truth;

Beareth all things, believeth all things, hopeth all things, endureth all things.

Charity never faileth: but whether there be prophecies, they shall fail; whether there be tongues, they shall cease; whether there be knowledge, it shall vanish away.

For we know in part, and we prophesy in part.

But when that which is perfect is come, then that which is in part shall be done away.

When I was a child, I spake as a child, I understood as a child, I thought as a child: but when I became a man, I put away childish things.

For now we see through a glass, darkly; but then face to face: now I know in part; but then shall I know even as also I am known.

And now abideth faith, hope, charity, these three; but the greatest of these is charity.

1 Corinthians 13

In the middle of the Apostle Paul's exposition on spiritual gifts in 1 Corinthians chapters 12 to 14 is the often quoted chapter on love: 1 Corinthians 13. While Paul recognizes the importance of the spiritual gifts and their place in the Christian's life, he tells that there is something superior to these gifts. Without charity (which is love) all other gifts have little value. In this month of February, often referred to the love month, let's take a look at the love chapter.

Love should penetrate every relationship we have, not just romantic and family relationships. Love is not confined to boyfriends and girlfriends. Love should be shown at work, the grocery store and in the church. 1 Peter 4:8 could be the background for my entire life; "And above all things have fervent charity among yourselves: for charity shall cover the multitude of sins." *The Power Is In The Love.* Not only is this my personal motto about love – it is also my life. I have learned (sometimes the hard way) that because of the anointing that God has placed upon my life that there are many people who are seeking to hurt or even destroy me. My reputation has been attacked, my family targeted, and my marriage assaulted. I have received threatening phone calls, I have been followed, and even had suspicious characters come to my job. Nonetheless – I still show love – even to the chagrin of those who love me.

Love must be mixed in with all the spiritual gifts. Paul specifically mentions the gifts of tongues, prophecy, knowledge, faith and giving. These gifts can't accomplish their purpose without the supremacy of love. Love is preeminent to all the spiritual gifts.

The two lists of what love is and isn't shows attitudes. Love is not just a word we say, but an attitude that we have towards others. Paul gives a succinct explanation of love that describes many of its attributes.

Love is:

- Patient
- Kind
- Rejoices in truth
- Bears up under all problems / Protects
- Believes / Trusts
- Hopes
- Understands the of faults of others

- Never fails / Perseveres

Love isn't:

- Envious
- Proud
- Boastful
- Inappropriate / Rude
- Selfish
- Short-tempered
- Evil
- Accepting of sin

There are various Greek words for love used in the Bible. The word used in this passage is the word agape which is the type of love God has towards us. It is a love that is not dependent on others; rather it is a personal choice. You can't make someone else have these qualities of love, but you can make a personal choice in your attitude toward them.

Even the enduring, permanent qualities of faith and hope will be of little value without love. While some of the spiritual gifts will be cut off or pass away, love will remain. One may have had the gift of prophecy or of knowledge, yet they wouldn't know all things. God does not reveal all things at one time to us. But there is a promise that "when that which is perfect is come, then that which is in part will be done away." Though some spiritual gifts will cease, there is always a need for love.

Love is permanent. Specifically he mentions that three items will continue and endure: faith, hope and love (or charity). Of the three, Paul says that love is superior. Even the enduring, permanent qualities of faith and hope will be of little value without love.

The motto, *"The Power Is In The Love"*, not only adorns my church building, but also my heart, mind, and attitude. There is true power in real love.

In their desire to receive gifts from God, the Corinthians were seeking the lesser gifts instead of the greater. Therefore, Paul begins this chapter by contrasting the worth of the spiritual gifts with the worth of love (13:1-3). Without love, the greatest gift is meaningless. He then defines love, by showing it in action, especially in the manner in which they should be using their spiritual gifts (13:4-7).

He concludes by emphasizing the eternal nature of love and the transitory nature of these spiritual gifts (13:8-13). The gifts were only designed to be temporary, as partial revelations until the whole was revealed. Love has always been the greatest thing—God is love (1 John 4:8), the Old Testament law and prophets hinged on love (Matthew

22:35-40) and love is the great commandment for us today (John 13:34-35).

Jesus said in John 13:35 *"By this shall all men know that ye are my disciples, if ye have love one to another."* Making the choice to love others is not only a suggestion given in 1 Corinthians 13, it is also a command given by our Lord to those who would call themselves Christians.

Questions To Ask Myself This Month

1. Are you loving? That may be a hard question to answer. It is very generic. But what about the qualities of love? Are you patient? Are you kind? Trusting?

_____

_____

_____

_____

2. Perhaps you possess these qualities now but previously did not. What (or who) changed you?

_____

_____

_____

_____

3. There is the other list too. Are you envious? Proud? Boastful? What about rude and short-tempered? How might you begin to change these things about yourself?

----

4. Often there are people who bring out certain qualities in us. Are you associating with the right people? Who in your life brings out your best qualities? Your worst?

Additional Notes

March

I'm Being Followed

The LORD is my shepard, I shall not want. He maketh me to lie down in green pastures: He leadeth me beside the still waters. He restoreth my soul: He leadeth me in the paths of righteousness for his name's sake. Yea, though I walk through the valley of the shadow of death, I will fear no evil: for thou art with me; thy rod and thy staff they comfort me. Thou preparest a table for me in the presence of my enimies. Thou annointest my head with oil; my cup runneth over. Surely goodness and mercy shall follow me in all the days of my life; and I will dwell in the house of the Lord forever.

Psalm 23

We live in a world in which many, if not most, people are engulfed with fear and anxiety. Some fear the future; they are anxious about what is going to happen. Others fear the past and they are anxious about what has happened. And still others fear even the present, anxiety has gripped their souls and they cannot imagine how they can cope with the ugliness of present circumstances in their lives. Thousands of people each day wake up with untold burdens to bear and anxiety with which they must deal. Are you one of these souls bearing secretly a heavy burden?

As a pastor I deal with hurting, anxious, and fearful souls on a daily basis. Despite what the public at large may believe I carry my sheep with me 24 hours a day. I do not preach a message on Sunday morning and go back to life as usual until the next Sunday. The Lord has entrusted me as an under-shepherd and I carry my sheep with me at all times; just as any good shepherd does.

On any given day my phone will ring beginning early morning (or in the middle of the night) with a secession of explosive and painful situations that my members are facing. A large portion of my day is spent responding to emails, fulfilling meeting requests and counseling sessions, and visiting with my sick and shut-in. It is not unusual for me be awake most of the night in intercessory prayer. My sheep carry such heavy burdens they may even find it difficult to release true praise and worship on Sunday morning.

How about you? Are you anxious for your finances? For many of us this is an area of tremendous concern especially in this unsteady economic atmosphere. However, sometimes we slip from concern into anxiety and are possessed with thoughts about the tentativeness of the security of our financial future. Some of you have children in college and you do not know how you're going to make ends meet as you continue to help them. Some of you have mortgage problems. Others have insurance problems and are anxious about what the future holds. Still there are many who have had their grown children move back home often with families of their own housing three or more generations in one home.

For some of us it's not finances, as much as it is simply worry about the future and where you're heading in life. You've graduated from college, you're married, but you still wonder where life is taking you or what it is that God really wants from you. As far as you know you're seeking Him and doing all that you know to do and have been taught to do. But still you're not sure about what's ahead.

The question then becomes, "How does God want me to respond to the anxiety in my life?" Well, like all the great questions of life, Scripture affords us an answer. This time it comes from the life of David. David says, by way of example, in Psalm 23, that there *is* a constructive, God-honoring way to respond to anxiety in our lives. He says that we should trust God as the good and faithful Shepherd and rejoice in His grace. Now, it must be said that responding to God in this way will not necessarily solve all of your financial problems, but God will provide confidence as to what He's doing in your life. He will convince you, as He did David, that it is He who is leading your life, He is the One who is in control of all the details and circumstances. This *will* lead to greater peace and knowledge that "we know that in all things God works for the good of those who love Him, who have been called according to His purpose." Let's take a closer look at the 23rd Psalm of David.

David was a man just like we are. He was tempted to fret over his life on many occasions, not the least of which was the period when Saul was seeking his life, which according to some commentators may very well form the background to this psalm. But you see, David overcame sinful worry by trusting and rejoicing in God. Psalm 23 then provides a model for us, a paradigm to be followed throughout our lives as we respond to all the difficulties and worries that come our way.

The psalm has two basic divisions, each one providing part of the answer to our question about worry. The first four verses focus on God as the faithful and good Shepherd of his people. It calls us to trust Him as such. The second section made up of the last two verses, focuses our attention on God as a gracious host, preparing a splendid meal for a guest, and results in our rejoicing over His grace toward us.

I. Trust God as the Good and Faithful Shepherd

A. To Provide for You

1. Yahweh is personal

So you see, David says in the first section, verses 1-4, that Yahweh is a faithful Shepherd and the last section, verses 5 and 6 that Yahweh is a gracious person. Let's talk about God as a Shepherd for a moment. There are three major things I want you to see about God as your Shepherd: 1) He provides for you (this is understood from verses 1-3a); 2) He guides you (verse 3b), and 3) He protects you (verse 4).

Focusing in on His provision first, we see three things emerge from the text. First, God is a personal Shepherd. David says the Lord is *my* Shepherd. David knew that the God of the universe was personal to Him and in control, as a good shepherd, of his whole life. The result of this, according to David, was the knowledge that he lacked nothing. Some versions say, "The Lord is my shepherd, I have everything I need." Like a good Shepherd the Lord gives Himself to us and therefore, we really lack nothing. The rest of verses 2-4 simply bear this out. How can we fail to trust a God who has so willingly made Himself available to us?

2. His provision is perfect

Second we see, in verse 2, that God's provision is perfect. David says that a good shepherd leads his sheep to green pastures and quiet waters. The green pastures probably refer to the tender young shoots that grow up in the morning and are loved by the wildlife of Palestine. The quiet waters may point to a well-spring with fresh water. The psalmist wants us to understand that this Shepherd goes all out for his sheep. The Shepherd wants them to have the best and is likewise sensitive to their needs. David wants us to understand that his God does the same for His people. It was David's experience and it ought to be ours. Some of us have deep struggles with our present situations, but we need to come to grips with the truth, that as we seek God, we are not getting second best from Him. He is a faithful Shepherd to give us only what is excellent according to His own purpose and agenda. Paul poses a question to us; "He that spared not his own Son, but delivered Him up for us all, how shall he not with him also freely give us all thing? (Romans 8:32).

3. His provision renews and satisfies (3a)

"He restoreth my soul." Many words in the Bible end with the suffix 'eth', most scholars believe and preach that 'eth' means a continual perpetuation of something or to be without end. For example, believeth means to continually believe. This is a powerful revelation in the understanding of the Lord as He "restoreth my soul".This should be understood first of all on the level of the metaphor of the sheep and its shepherd. Therefore, we could say that the green pastures and quiet waters, provided by so caring a shepherd are for the physical nourishment and energy of the sheep. The shepherd literally revives the life of the sheep under his care.

God's provision for David and for us accomplishes similar ends. Whether it is physical needs that are met or spiritual, it revives or rebuilds us - continually. Ultimately it strengthens our trust in God and enlivens our spiritual sensitivities toward Him. It satisfies our longings to receive from His hand.

4. Conclusion

So you see it is reasonable to trust our faithful Shepherd. His provision is always perfect and renews and satisfies us. Rather than worry ourselves to death, why not trust God for what only He can provide? God's faithful provision is only part of what He does for those who know and love Him. He guides them as well. Look at verse 3b.

B. To Guide You

"He guides me in paths of righteousness for His name's sake." I want you to notice two things here: 1) He guides you in righteous paths and 2) He does it for His name's sake.

1. He guides you in righteous paths

David goes on to say that as we go through life God guides us, as a good shepherd, along paths of righteousness. For the sheep, of course, this means right or true paths; paths that are certain to lead to the places of rest and provision talked about in verse 2. But for David, God desired to lead him down paths of uprightness during his kingship and enable him to win great battles in his commission to possess the land promised to the nation. God desires to lead us into greater and greater righteousness in our lives as well. We should be concerned about this. Paul says in 1 Thessalonians 4:7 that God has not called us for the purpose of impurity, but in sanctification or holiness and that God's intention is to sanctify us entirely"

2. He guides you for His name's sake

The end of verse 3 gives the reason why God was such a faithful Shepherd to David and still is for us today. He does it for His own name's sake. That is, it is for the sake of the glory and reputation of His own name and honor. What kind of reputation would a shepherd in Palestine earn if everyone knew he was careless and irresponsible with his own sheep? What kind of reputation would God earn for Himself if He were careless with those who belong in His charge? God's name is on the line in your life. He wants to show the world that He is faithful to provide for all your needs and guide you in righteous paths, in a holy life.

The shepherd must also protect his sheep. This is the focus of verse 4.

C. To Protect You

David says, "…though I walk through the valley of the shadow of death, I will fear no evil; for Thou art with me; Thy rod and Thy staff, they comfort me." Taken literally the phrase "valley of the shadow of death" most likely refers to deep ravines with sharp cliffs. And, it was not at all uncommon in Palestine for a shepherd to have to travel through one of these dark ravines where danger was imminent (i.e. either from the cliffs themselves or from animals hiding and waiting for their prey), in order to get to another food source. And so it is with life. We often travel through what appears to be dangerous circumstances— perhaps David is thinking of the attempts made on his life by Saul and others—but we need not be overcome with fear for as the shepherd is with us and is able to ward off any danger by his rod and staff, so God is powerful enough to protect us from danger.

There is no such claim that God will shield us from every harmful circumstance—this is patently false as many of us can testify—but that 1) nothing can separate us from Christ during those experiences (Romans 8:38,39) and 2) that He alone passes approval on what things are permitted to afflict us and 3) it really is for our good and deeper knowledge of Him (Romans 8:28). You can trust Him to protect you from everything that desires to kill, steal, or destroy you (John 10:10).

D. Summary

God is a faithful Shepherd. He provides for us without sparing a single detail. He guides us into a righteous life for the sake of His own reputation and He protects us, not by shielding us from difficulty, though He does at times, but by permitting in our lives only what is beneficial to us according to His good purpose for us. We need to trust Him as our faithful shepherd.

II. Rejoice in God's grace

A. Because He Spares no Blessing (5)

The picture here is of God as a gracious host, throwing a banquet as it were, sparing no extravagance for the invited guest. David says, "my cup overflows" which could either mean that the quality of the drink is absolutely superb or that the host had provided him with an abundance. Either way, the tremendous grace of God is evident in David's experience here.

B. Because it Results in Constant Fellowship with Him (6)

He says, in verse 6, "Surely (notice David's confidence) goodness and mercy shall follow me in all the days of my life." Rather than being pursued by his enemies (e.g. Saul), the goodness and mercy (i.e. God's lovingkindness) of God will follow him all his days and he knows that he will dwell in the house of the Lord for as long as he lives.

Earlier we read about the "shadow of death". Shadows are tricky and carry the illusion of danger and foreboding. We tend to think of shadows as dark, frightening places where all manner of evil lurks. But let us understand that a shadow is not a darkness, it is instead, an area that is blocked from light because of an object in its path. The Lord has shined His light so brightly *on* you and *through* you that evil takes cover *behind* you, in your shadow. It is not hiding *in* the dark; it is hiding *from* the light. Scary, isn't it? *BUT*, "**surely** <u>GOODNESS</u> and <u>MERCY</u> shall follow me." Evil may stand in my shadow but God's light is shining on me and goodness and mercy are behind me – whom shall I fear? (Psalm 27:1)

David envisions the direction his life will take as centered around fellowship and communion with his God. The grace of God can accomplish that in our lives as well. Do we realize how gracious God has been to us in Christ, forgiving our sin against Him and giving us His Spirit to enable us to walk with Him (1 Corinthians 2:12)? We ought to rejoice in God's grace toward us, rather than be overcome with anxiety over the circumstances the good Shepherd allows in our lives.

Questions To Ask Myself This Month

1. David knew the Lord as his shepherd. In what ways has the Lord shepherded you in your life? In this month? This day?

_____

_____

_____

_____

2. We want to know that God is our Shepherd, but we tolerate sin in our lives. It goes unconfessed for long periods of time. We must confess our sins and permit God, as our faithful shepherd to deal with us. What sins are you hiding from? Why haven't you confessed them?

_____

_____

_____

3. How should you respond to problems and pain in your life?

_____

_____

_____

_____

4. Dealing with a large and daunting situation can sometimes cause us to feel overwhelmed which, in turn, leaves us fearful, anxious, and exhausted. To avoid this we must try not to let situations get out of hand in the first place. What are some of the "little" things in your daily life that cause you irritations? How might our deal with the "little" things before they become "big" things?

_____

_____

_____

_____

5. The Hebrew word often translated "follow" is actually closer in meaning to the word "pursue": "Goodness and mercy will pursue me." Why would God pursue us? Do you feel this happening in your life?

_____

_____

_____

_____

6. Do you see "dwelling in the house of the Lord" as a heavenly or an earthly state? Is there a difference?

_____

_____

_____

_____

Additional Notes

April
Step Out On Faith

But without faith it is impossible to please him: for he that cometh to God must believe that he is, and that he is a rewarder of them that diligently seek him.

Hebrews 11:6

What exactly is faith? How do we know we have it? If we have it, do we have enough? What good thing happens if we have faith? Hebrews 11 is one of the great chapters of the Bible dealing with faith. Few chapters rival it in terms of influence and spiritual power.

The Assurance of Faith –

The structure of chapter 11 is clear. Verses 1-3 provide a general introduction to the subject of faith. Verses 4-7 focus on the faith of three major characters up to the Flood: Noah, Enoch, and Abel. Verses 8-22 deal with Abraham while verses 23-28 point to Moses as the example of faith.

Hebrews 11:1-3

There is no break in the author's flow of thought from Hebrews 10:38-39 to chapter 11. Verse 39 described the readers as "them that believe to the saving of the soul." Hebrews 11:1-3 then defines that faith, not philosophically or technically, but descriptively.

Verse 1 defines faith as *the substance of things hoped for, the evidence of things not seen.* The New Testament word faith is used with a variety of meanings. The noun, faith, and the verb, "to believe," come from the same Greek root and the two words are closely related. Faith or believing can mean nothing more than the acknowledgment of a fact. James 2:19 comments that the demons believe that God is one and tremble over that fact. However, in the New Testament the words point to a personal commitment.

The English word *trust* may be a better translation of the Greek. *Trust* is both a noun and verb and it speaks of investment or commitment of oneself. The substance of things hoped for is confident, serene trust in God.

The idea of substance (translated assurance) has already been used in Hebrews. It appeared first in Hebrews 1:3 pointing to the very being of God himself. It was used again in Hebrews 3:14 to describe the first "confidence" that the readers had possessed. Thus in Hebrews 1:3 the word refers to the objective reality of God. It is quite likely that the author wants us to understand the reality (objectively) of things hoped for lies in confident trust in God. That reality provides an assurance (subjectively felt by the believer) that the things hoped for are on the way. Thus confident trust in God gives the things we hope for "all the reality of present existence; and irresistibly convinces us of the reality of things unseen and brings us into their presence."

It is important for us to remember the New Testament understanding of faith at this point. It was not because Abraham was a spiritual superman that he obeyed God. It was because he trusted God that he made a life decision to obey.

The faith that Hebrews calls for is not a warm fuzzy feeling, it is not spiritual power. The faith Hebrews calls for is simply trusting God enough to obey his will. Pastor Sheryl Brady likes to define faith as "a calm assurance that the Lord will make everything alright." What a blessed assurance indeed!

The original readers of Hebrews were called upon to trust God enough to continue their commitment to Christ in the face of persecution. We are called upon to trust God enough to obey him when we face pressure to compromise or abandon our commitment.

So let us now move on to our focus text which is verse 6. Coming to God means that we must believe that He is and that He can. What would be the point of coming to Him if we did not really believe that He could provide for us? So we are to believe that He is. He is what? God uses many words and phrases to describe himself throughout the Bible. They are commonly called the I Am's Of God. Here are just a few.

- I AM
- I AM THAT I AM
- I AM a father to Israel
- I AM a great king
- I AM God Almighty
- I AM gracious
- I AM He
- I AM he that comforteth you
- I AM the God of Abraham, and the God of Isaac, and the God of Jacob
- I AM the first and the last
- I AM the Lord thy God
- I AM thy salvation
- I AM thy shield
- I AM the bread of life
- I AM the light of the world
- I AM the true vine
- I AM the door of the sheep
- I AM the resurrection, and the life

My son is an attorney. Lawyers like to speak of the "elements" of proof in litigation. That is, what do you have to prove to make out your case in court? What are the elements of proof of a "saving faith?" (This text lays out two elements: first, we must believe God exists; and, second, we must believe that He rewards those who come to Him.)

What does it mean to believe that God "rewards" those who come to Him? Does it mean we will get rich? We will marry well? We will be famous? We will have good health? Our children will obey? (This idea is very interesting and important. It teaches us that faith is not simply believing in God, but our belief must have an impact on how we live. The Hebrew word translated "rewards" literally means "to give back wages." "Payback" is another way to say this. There is a saying that goes "work for God, the pay is low and the hours are long, but the benefits are out of this world."

I invite you to step forward in faith. To believe that God exists and to earnestly seek Him who rewards those who come to Him.

Questions To Ask Myself This Month

1. What kind of faith are you beginning to desire in your own heart?

_____

_____

_____

_____

2. A question we can ask ourselves is, "Can we be saved without faith in God?" Regardless of your answer to that, consider this; what do you perceive salvation to be?

_____

_____

_____

_____

3. What kind of rewards are you expecting from God? How do/will you react if you don't get them?

_____

_____

_____

_____

4. Even Abraham, a noted pillar of faith, struggled at times. Abraham and Sarah both laughed at the promises of God, at one point even trying to get God to accept Abraham's son with Hagar as the fulfillment of that promise. How have you lost faith (even unintentionally) of God's promises for your life? Did you try to 'help God along'?

_____

_____

_____

_____

Additional Notes

May

Smooth Criminal

The thief cometh not, but for to steal, and to kill, and to destroy: I am come that they might have life, and that they might have it more abundantly. John 10:10

When we think of a thief we usually think of a shady character of little moral value seeking to rob upstanding individuals of the things they have worked so hard to obtain. Thieves use intimidation, threat and violence to take what they want. The thief works under cover of darkness in an attempt to not be caught. Thieves will destroy whatever it is their path without conscience. They are loathsome, they are dastardly, they are ungodly. Sound familiar? Thieves do not care about their victims. Neither does the enemy.

In order to understand what John 10:10 means, we need to look at its context. Chapter 10 of John's Gospel develops the biblical theme of sheep and the shepherd as we looked at in the month of March. The shepherd is accessible to the sheep. Strangers do not have a personal relationship with the flock, but the shepherd does. Verse 10 draws the contrast between Jesus and false shepherds, the thieves who come to kill, steal and destroy.

Let's look at the first six verses of John 10.

Verily, verily, I say unto you, He that entereth not by the door into the sheepfold, but climbeth up some other way, the same is a thief and a robber. But he that entereth in by the door is the shepherd of the sheep. To him the porter openeth; and the sheep hear his voice: and he calleth his own sheep by name, and leadeth them out. And when he putteth forth his own sheep, he goeth before them, and the sheep follow him: for they know his voice. And a stranger will they not follow, but will flee from him: for they know not the voice of strangers. This parable spake Jesus unto them: but they understood not what things they were which he spake unto them.

What do you think of the depiction above? How much of it is figurative and how much literal? All of it is literal. Jesus is describing a sheepfold in a town, where the sheep of visiting shepherds are kept together. When a shepherd is ready to leave town again, he returns to the sheepfold and calls out his sheep, who recognize his voice and follow through the gate, which the doorkeeper opens. Individual flocks in the region were not thousands of animals but small enough for the shepherds to know their sheep individually and even name them like we name our pets. The context of this passage is the continuation of Jesus' words to the Pharisees at the end of chapter 9. He is saying that their inability to understand or follow Him shows that they don't belong to God. Since they don't understand, He shifts to another analogy. As a pastor, this is significant to me because there are times I feel my sheep do not understand or are not 'following' me. In these cases I must also switch my strategy or approach in order to help them recognize the shepherd's voice.

In John 10:7 and John 10:9, Jesus calls Himself a door; once again, this is literal. What Jesus is now describing is a shepherd's own sheep pen, which was either a cave or a fenced-in area with a gap in the fence. Once the sheep had been brought into the sheep pen for the night, the shepherd lay and slept across the mouth of the cave or the gap in the fence so that no sheep can leave or predator enter without awaking him; he literally served as the door of the sheep pen.

The door metaphor is then turned around in verses 9-10. Here Jesus is the door by which the sheep go out to find pasture, salvation, and life. There is no other way by which the sheep can find these benefits. If they do not come through Christ, they will not find life and salvation. If they are fooled into following the thieves they will not find the life that is salvation for John. If they follow the thief they will find death and destruction. This is another beautiful picture of Jesus. It clearly teaches that he is the only way for salvation. Verse 10 concludes this section with a statement of Jesus' purpose. *"I am come that they might have life, and that they might have it more abundantly."* The purpose of life echoes John's purpose statement for the whole book found in John 20:31. *"But these are written, that ye might believe that Jesus is the Christ, the Son of God; and that believing ye might have life through his name."*

And what about the life to be had more abundantly in John 10:10? Jesus is talking about eternal life in heaven, not a materialistically abundant life on earth, which can be had without Jesus. Jeremiah 12:1 says: *"You are always righteous, LORD, when I bring a case before you. Yet I would speak with you about your justice: Why does the way of the wicked prosper? Why do all the faithless live at ease?"* *(NIV).* How many times have we been confounded or angry at a person who seems to have everything but a relationship with Jesus while we toil and spin and seem to get nowhere?

John 10:1-6 - The Sheep, the Shepherd, and Sheep Robbers

These opening verses introduce the figures of speech from shepherding that will be used in the first part of chapter 10. Again Jesus' use of sheep imagery has a strong Old Testament background. Psalm 23 is the best-known Old Testament passage to use sheep and shepherd figuratively for spiritual purposes. It is more likely that Jesus was drawing upon Ezekiel 34 in his metaphorical use of sheep language. The background of Ezekiel 34 is especially important for John 10:1-18. Ezekiel described Israel as God's flock and the rulers (kings) as the shepherds. Rather than feeding the sheep, the rulers alternately ignore the flock and actually prey upon them instead of protecting them. As a result the flock is scattered and devoured by the wild animals. The false shepherds will be removed from their position of leadership and God will again be the shepherd of his people. He will gather them and lead them to good pasture. He will appoint a shepherd over them from David's line and bring peace to the flock. Ezekiel 34 is a startlingly clear description of the way Jesus portrayed himself as the good shepherd. Powerful picture isn't it?

Verses 1-3 describe the proper way to approach the sheep. It is through the door or gate of the sheepfold. That is the way the shepherd comes to the sheep. Anyone who approaches another way has evil intentions. Verses 3-5 focus more on the close relationship between the sheep and the shepherd. The shepherd knows his sheep and calls his own sheep by name. I find it amazing that I can say "Jesus?" and he will say "Yes, Jackie"? My shepherd knows me and I him. I follow at the sound of his voice and will not follow a stranger.

Some of us may feel insulted at the thought of being compared to a sheep. Due to their strong flocking instinct and failure to act independently of one another, sheep have been universally branded "stupid." But sheep are not stupid. Their only protection from predators is to band together and follow the sheep in front of them. If a predator is threatening the flock, this is not the time to act independently. In turn, if we are to be protected from our enemies we must not only band together but we must know and follow our shepherd.

So who is the thief? How is the thief trying to destroy us? The solemn "truly, truly" of verse 1 combined with a description of everyday shepherding experience suggests a parable. In verse 6 John declares that Jesus spoke this as a figure of speech or a proverb. They did not understand. This reference to "they" brings us back to the question of the audience. Within the literary flow of the gospel the Jewish leaders of chapter 9 form that audience. If we consider John 10:1-5 in isolation from chapter 9 our sympathy lies with those Jewish leaders. Looking only at these five verses it is very hard to know what Jesus means by the figurative references to shepherding. This is why it is imperative to look at every aspect of a scripture before making a judgment on it and why I take the time to expound every verse we are studying.

The context of chapter 9 and going back to the background of Ezekiel 34 make the parable(s) much clearer. Jesus is accusing those Jewish religious leaders of being false shepherds. They are the thieves and robbers mentioned in verse 1. He is the shepherd whose voice the sheep follow. They are the strangers - the rustlers who care nothing for the sheep but only for the profit they can make for themselves from the sheep.

As is often the case with the parables of Jesus, misunderstanding is not just a matter of intellectual puzzlement.

The real reason those religious leaders do not understand the parable is their own hard heartedness, arrogance and ignorance. They refuse to allow the parable to expose their own sinfulness and need of God. When that is the purpose of a parable and one refuses to accept that possibility it becomes difficult to find any other meaning.

There are two different applications of the door metaphor in verses 7-10. Verse 8 interprets Jesus as the door by which the shepherd comes to the sheep. The thieves and robbers did not come through Jesus, the door, to get at the sheep. The fact that they used other means proves that they are imposters. If Jesus is the door by which the authentic shepherd comes to the sheep then Jesus is not the shepherd at this point, but God is. Verses 7-8 seem to be saying that Jesus is the door by which God comes to shepherd us. This view assumes the background of Ezekiel 34 where God is the shepherd of Israel. This is a beautiful picture of the Incarnation. It is God who comes to care for us through Jesus. Mind blowing isn't it?

The door metaphor is then turned around in verses 9-10. Here Jesus is the door by which the sheep go out to find pasture, salvation, and life. There is no other way by which the sheep can find these benefits. If they do not come through Christ, they will not find life and salvation. If they are fooled into following the thieves they will not find the life that is salvation for John. If they follow the thief they will find death and destruction. This is another beautiful picture of Jesus. It clearly teaches that he is the only way for salvation. Verse 10 concludes this section with a statement of Jesus' purpose. I came in order that they might have life and that they might have it in abundance. The purpose of life echoes John's purpose statement for the whole book found in John 20:30-31. These things have been written in order that you might believe . . . and that when you have believed you might have life in his name.

Jesus' main purpose was the salvation (health) of the sheep, which he defined as free access to pasture and fullness of life. Under his protection and by his gift they can experience the best life can offer. In the context of John's emphasis on eternal life, this statement takes on new significance. Jesus can give a whole new meaning to living because he provides full satisfaction and perfect guidance.

Barclay's Daily Study Bible adds,

Jesus claims that he came that men might have life and might have it more abundantly. The Greek phrase used for having it more abundantly means to have a superabundance of a thing.

To be a follower of Jesus, to know who he is and what he means, is to have a superabundance of life. A Roman soldier came to Julius Caesar with a request for permission to commit suicide. He was a wretched dispirited creature with no vitality. Caesar looked at him. "Man," he said, "were you ever really alive?" When we try to live our own lives, life is a dull, dispirited thing. When we walk with Jesus, there comes a new vitality, a superabundance of life. It is only when we live with Christ that life becomes really worth living and we begin to live in the real sense of the word.

Questions To Ask Myself This Month

1. When reading the parables, indeed all the teaching, of Jesus, we need to be asking, "What does this reveal about me?" "Do I need to be different?" "What does God want to do in changing my attitudes, thoughts, and life?"

_____

_____

_____

_____

2. Do you have abundant life? If not, what must you do to receive it?

_____

_____

_____

_____

3. How can we know the difference between God's voice and the voice of the "wisdom of the world"?

_____

_____

_____

_____

4. Think of a time when you followed the shepherd's voice. Where did it lead you? Have you ever mistakenly followed the thief's voice? Where did it lead you?

_____

_____

_____

_____

Additional Notes

_____

_____

_____

_____

_____

_____

_____

_____

_____

_____

_____

_____

_____

_____

_____

_____

June

The Power Of Thanksgiving

In every thing give thanks: for this is the will of God in Christ Jesus concerning you. 1 Thessalonians 5:18

This is a powerful verse that is often misquoted and misunderstood. The scripture implores us to give thanks *in* all things, not *for* all things. This means that we give thanks in spite of all the things that may come against us. We do not thank God for trouble; we thank Him regardless of it. I have serious back issues due to arthritis. My left leg is numb most of the time. I have little, in any, cartilage left in my knees. Despite these things I give the Lord praise and thanks every day and in everything. I don't thank God for my pain but I thank Him in it.

We can give thanks "in everything" because we know that "all things work together for good to them that love God" (Romans 8:28). God ordains adversity as well as prosperity. Every circumstance that comes our way is from God. We can give thanks for everything because God is in control. Neither do we give thanks necessarily "after" everything. It does not require much faith to trace the hand of God with the benefit of hindsight. However, it takes faith to accept one's lot with gratitude in the midst of circumstances.

"...Giving thanks always for all things unto God and the Father in the name of our Lord Jesus Christ;..." (Ephesians 5:20).

This passage in Ephesians is more powerful than our verse in Thessalonians. We are to give thanks always for all things. When the police call and tell you that your son is in jail, it is difficult to give thanks for that. But we need to have the attitude of Samuel in 1 Samuel 3:18,

"...So Samuel told him everything, hiding nothing from him. Then Eli said, "He is the LORD; let him do what is good in his eyes." (NIV)

Whatever comes in our lives comes in by the will of God, otherwise, He would prevent it. God mixes with His divine compound the bitter and the sweet, the good and the bad, in appropriate proportions so that they work together for good. God knows just the right amount of sunshine and rain. He measures out these things with great precision.

Conventional wisdom tells us that nothing is certain except death and taxes, but for most of us that is not enough. Wouldn't you like to be just as sure about where you stand with God? That's what the Thessalonians were looking for, and Paul's letters to them can help us find that assurance as well.

In the year A.D. 50, Paul entered Thessalonica while on his second missionary journey. He preached there for three weeks and was able to establish a church. However, a group of jealous Jews interpreted Paul's message to mean that he was proclaiming another ruler in opposition to the Roman emperor, and he was forced to leave town (Acts 17:1-10).

Because of Paul's concern for this young church, he sent his co-laborer and mentee, Timothy, to learn how the Thessalonians were doing. Timothy reported that the Christians' faith remained strong but that they continued to be persecuted by those who had banished Paul. Timothy also brought back questions which Paul had not had time to answer during his short stay.

First Thessalonians was Paul's first attempt at offering encouragement and answering questions—in fact research suggests it was probably the first of Paul's epistles. It was written from Corinth only a few months after Paul had left Thessalonica. Like the church we also tend to face adversity while attempting to keep our faith strong.

No matter what is happening in your life, you can be thankful. The Bible gives us a long list of things we should be thankful for. These are the things that never change, no matter what is happening in your life. We are to be thankful:

- That God is good (1 Chronicles 16:34)

- That His love lasts forever (Psalm 106:1)

- For God's amazing grace (1 Corinthians 1:11)

- For the wonderful things God does (Psalm 107:8)

- Because God answers prayers (Psalm 118:21)

- For His perfect laws (Psalm 119:62)

- Because God gives us wisdom and reveals His truth to us (Daniel 2:22-23)

- For other believers (Philippians 1:3)

And most of all, we should be thankful because God gave His Son, Jesus, to save us from the punishment of our sin, and give us new life! (1 Corinthians 15:57) God has saved all who believe in Jesus; He has taken our sin and given us His righteousness.

The Bible says that being thankful brings honor to God (Psalm 50:23). God actually commands us to be thankful. Back in the Old Testament, there were certain sacrifices that people were instructed to make as thank offerings to the Lord. When we thank God, we acknowledge that He deserves the credit. He has done for us what we could not do for ourselves. When others see you thank God, you point them to Him.

Giving thanks also helps us, because it makes us focus our attention back to the One we are thanking! Giving thanks helps you focus on God. It will remind you that God is in control of everything. He never changes and He only allows what is good for you. You can have FAITH in God's goodness, and not FEAR the things around you. No matter what is happening in your life, give thanks to God in the middle of your circumstances. His grace is abundant, His love for you lasts forever, and He gives new life to everyone who trusts in Him.

Questions To Ask Myself This Month

1. In 1 Thessalonians Paul offers encouragement in four major areas: (1) How can I be sure that I will be with Jesus after death? (2) How can I be sure that Jesus is coming again? (3) How can I be sure that Jesus hasn't forgotten me when I am suffering persecution? (4) How can I be sure that my life is pleasing to God?

_____

_____

_____

_____

_____

_____

_____

_____

2. What situations have you found yourself in when it was difficult to give God thanks?

_____

_____

_____

_____

_____

3. Paul instructs the Thessalonians to "rejoice" "pray" and "give thanks" (1 Thess 5:16-18). How are you doing in these three categories? If you are weak in these areas, how can you strengthen these characteristics in your walk with the Lord?

_____

_____

_____

_____

Additional Notes

July
Being a Do-Gooder

And the LORD shall make thee the head, and not the tail; and thou shalt be above only, and thou shalt not be beneath; if that thou hearken unto the commandments of the LORD thy God, which I command thee this day, to observe and to do them: And thou shalt not go aside from any of the words which I command thee this day, to the right hand, or to the left, to go after other gods to serve them. Deuteronomy 28:13-14

This chapter is a very large exposition of two words, the blessing and the curse. They are real things and have real effects. The blessings are here put before the curses. God is slow to anger, but swift to show mercy. Beloved, it is his delight to bless us. The blessing is promised, upon condition that we diligently hearken to the voice of God. Let them keep up their faith, the form and power of it, in their families and nation, then the providence of God would prosper all their outward concerns. Fire, when introduced to gun power will explode. In turn; seed, when sewn into good soil will bear fruit,"... for whatsoever a man soweth, that shall he also reap." (Gal. 6:7)

This scripture can easily be used to describe a good man or what the Lord ultimately expects from us. The good man is described by his teachable spirit. He "hearkens diligently unto the voice of the Lord." He has a sense of need, a sense of dependence upon another. He admits God's right to instruct and to command. He inquires after God, and reverently listens to his voice. It is his delight to hear the wise instructions of the unerring God.

He is described by his circumspection. He is observant of God's ways, discovers manifold and hidden indications of His will. Not only is his ear intent to the whispers of his Father, but his eye is open too. Blindness of mind has gone.

He is described by his completeness of obedience. He practically "does all the commandments of God." These came of old by the agency of Moses; but a good man detects within the human voice the Divine message - the authority of Heaven. And his entire conduct is determined by the known will of God.

The Greek philosopher Aristotle once said, "If you prove the cause, you at once prove the effect; and conversely nothing can exist without its cause." In this case the effect is blessing and the cause is obedience. "The Lord thy God will set thee on high above all nations of the earth." As in nature it is certain that all botanical life shoots upward, or that gases, as they expand, also ascend; so in the spiritual kingdom it is certain that goodness will grow into eminence. The character of God is a guarantee that the constitutional principles of his kingdom do not change. Faithful service shall be crowned with honor.

The reward of goodness truly is its own permanence. "The Lord shall establish thee an holy people" (verse 9). "And thou shalt not go aside from any of the words which I command thee." In the life of obedience "God helps those who help themselves." Separate acts become easier by repetition. They evolve into habits. Habits lead to permanence, permanence becomes character, and character determines your destiny.

Behind all forms of blessing a personal God can be seen. The material food of this world does not sustain bodily life; it is God acting through the food. Neither fertile land, nor good husbandry, nor auspicious weather, nor all combined, will in themselves secure a plentiful harvest; it is only by the will and pleasure of God. "The Lord shall command the blessing." However riches may increase, if God smile not, there will be no joy. The house may be full of children; yet instead of great health there may be terrible sickness - instead of intellectual energy, stupidity - instead of laughter, weeping. We may possess substantial homes, yet no security; thieves and murderers may infest the land, True prosperity is a Divine Father's blessing.

A good man also delights in *doing* good. He enjoys being a blessing to those around him and petitions the Lord to increase him that he may accomplish this goal. "Thou shalt lend, and shalt not borrow." The Name of God is put upon him. He acts in God's stead, and imitates God in all things. The result of the Divine favor will be evident. All people will see the gracious distinction which marks and signalizes us as friends of God. All his deeds will be covered with a glory not born of earth. His influence will spread far and wide. He becomes a " He was a burning and a shining light: and ye were willing for a season to rejoice in his light." (John 5:35)

You will be abundantly blessed for your obedience. There is no question of this. God is not a man that he should lie neither the son of man that he should repent; this being so if God has promised that he will bless us according to our obedience should we not believe him? I know I do.

Questions To Ask Myself This Month

1. How many of us have hoped and prayed for a financial blessing? Some of us have even gone to extremes to gain it. Did you receive the blessing? If so, what did you do with it?

_____

_____

_____

_____

2. Are you the head of anything? This can include a position on your job, in the church, in your neighborhood, etc.? How did you obtain that position? Did you seek it or was it placed upon you?

_____

_____

_____

_____

_____

3. Sometimes we do feel like "the tail". We feel like we are at the bottom or beneath others. Describe a time when you felt that way. Compose a specific prayer to the Lord to help you overcome that feeling.

_____

_____

_____

_____

_____

_____

4. Matthew chapter 7 speaks of false prophets and assures us we will know them by their fruits. A good tree bears good fruit and a bad tree bears bad fruit. We also are known by our works. How do those around you know you? What would your friends, family, and co-workers say about you?

_____

_____

_____

_____

Additional Notes

_____

_____

_____

_____

_____

_____

_____

_____

_____

_____

_____

_____

_____

_____

_____

August
The Weapons Of Our Warfare

No weapon that is formed against thee shall prosper; and every tongue that shall rise against thee in judgment thou shalt condemn. This is the heritage of the servants of the LORD, and their righteousness is of me, saith the LORD. Isaiah 54:17

We as Christians face many attacks by satan, we are attacked through temptations, accusation, sickness, and deception. But during the storm we must believe that God's got our back. He has a plan for our lives and will not leave us alone or unprotected.

Above all else I am a musician at heart and there is nothing I love more than to praise my God with my gift of music. My time behind my keyboard is my time to use my anointing and my gifting together. In music terminology a movement is a separate section of a larger composition. There are three movements in this scripture:

1. Devil's instruments - He attacks with 3 weapons.

    A. weapons of words-slander, lies.

    B. Weapons of works-evil deeds done against us.

    C. weapons of the world-drugs, alcohol.

2. Innocence - We are under attack not because we have done wrong but because we are right (righteous). The devil and his imps have declared war on the church.

3. Insurance - But God has told us that we will be alright because no weapon formed against us shall prosper. God has got your back, so we need not worry about the enemies attack.

"In righteousness shalt thou be established: thou shalt be far from oppression." (verse 14) Many Holy Ghost filled children of God are allowing themselves to be oppressed. Oppression is the spoiling or taking away of someone's goods or rights unlawfully by force, fear or deceitfulness - taking advantage of weakness or fearfulness. I think that describes satan to a tee. He is the oppressor, but Acts 10:38 says that Jesus healed all that were oppressed of the devil. The righteousness that Isaiah spoke of has been established. Jesus came and provided it for us. The very message Jesus preached was you don't have to fear any more.

The next line in this verse is extremely powerful: "For thou shalt not fear." I have an acronym for fear;

False

Evidence

Appearing

Real

The Bible says fear has torment.

I John 4:18. There is no fear in love; but perfect love casteth out fear, because fear hath torment, he that feareth is not made perfect in love.

II Timothy 1:7. For God hath not given us the spirit of fear, but of power and of love, and of a sound mind.

Psalms 23:4. Yea though I walk through the valley of the shadow of death I will fear no evil, for thou art with me, thy rod and thy staff they comfort me.

Adam's first statement after his meeting with the devil was, "I was afraid." Do you know that every time we fear we are doubting at least one of God's promises? Fear moves us into doubt and opens the door for Satan to work. II Peter 1:1-4 tells us that God's promises cover all things that pertain to life and godliness.

Does this mean we should never fear? Certainly not. It means that through the work of Jesus at Calvary we can choose to live by faith or live by fear. If we don't come against fear in our lives, it will consume us. The Bible says the just shall live by faith. Fear not. That phrase appears over 60 times in the Word of God. Fear is faith in reverse. It is believing for the worst. It is expecting God's Word to fail. It is doubt at its fullest.

Let's look at verse 15. They shall gather together, but not by me. They who? The ones we were just talking about. The great thieves of God's blessings: oppression and fear. The Lord is saying these will gather together around you, but they are not of me. These things come our way, but we don't have to surrender to them. If these spirits are gathering against you, God didn't send them. He is not the God of oppression or fear. In fact, he said, "Whosoever shall gather together against thee shall fall for thy sake." When fear gripped Jehoshophat, he set himself to seek the Lord and found courage in the promises of God. Jehoshophat said, "Lord, I know you are going to hear and to help because your name is in this house."

Look at verse 15 again."Whosoever shall gather together against thee shall fall for thy sake." Where there is fear, there is doubt. Doubt will stop the flow of blessing in your life. Mark 11:23-24 is only promised to the one who does not doubt in his heart. "For verily I say unto you that whosoever shall say unto this mountain be thou removed and be thou cast into the sea; and shall not doubt in his heart, but shall believe that those things which he saith shall come to pass; he shall have whatsoever he saith, therefore, I say unto you, what things soever ye desire, when ye pray, believe that ye receive them, and ye shall have them."

He said, when you pray, believe ye receive, not when you see it, but when you pray it. There is no receiving outside of believing. If you ever received, someone believed. Fear and unbelief robbed Israel (God's chosen people) from entering into the Promised Land. Hebrews 4:6 says the ones the gospel was first preached to entered not in because of unbelief.

This is a very important lesson from the scripture; why some things don't get finished in our lives. In the 14th chapter of Matthew the disciples were out on the sea in a boat and in the 4th watch of the night Jesus came walking on the sea. They were fearful, but Peter said, "Lord, if it be thou, bid me come unto thee on the water." Jesus said, "Come." Now the Bible says that when Peter was come down out of the ship, he walked on the water to go to Jesus. Jesus began a miraculous supernatural thing in Peter's life, but it was never consummated. It never came to full fruit. Why?

Because when Peter looked at the waves and the wind, his heart believed what he saw instead of what Jesus said.

Fear and doubt robbed him of the greater blessing. We can choose to believe what we see or believe what God has said.

Jesus saved Peter and brought him back to the boat. Jesus still loved him, but fear and doubt had robbed him of the greater blessing.

Peter was close to Jesus; one of his closest followers, but doubt had robbed him. Doubt will come to rob you, even if you are close to Jesus. Jesus said to Peter, "Oh, thou of little faith. A little faith carried him a little ways. As long as Peter considered Jesus and acted on what Jesus said, the supernatural was operating in his life. As soon as he took his eyes off Jesus, he began to sink.

Our study verse says, Isaiah 54:17, says; "No weapon formed against you shall prosper; and every tongue that shall rise against you in judgment thou shalt condemn. This is the heritage of the servants of the Lord, and their righteousness is of me saith the Lord."

This is a promise of God. God's Word is a weapon against fear. The Bible says in Matthew 11:28: "Come to me all ye who are weary and I will give you rest." Lay down your fear, cast aside your oppression and let Him give you rest. The weapons of the enemy are strong but as long as the Lord is on our side the weapons of the enemy cannot and will not prosper.

Questions To Ask Myself This Month

1. The enemy uses many weapons in his quest to destroy the people of God. What are some of the weapons he has used against you? How did you fire back?

_____

_____

_____

_____

2. Some people mistakenly believe that because we are promised that no weapon formed will prosper that we are somehow invincible. There are people who drink poison, handle deadly snakes, and do all manner of dangerous things. This is not trusting God, is it testing God. Have you ever tested God's limits? How far did you go? What brought you back?

_____

_____

_____

_____

3. God has not given us the spirit of fear. What are you afraid of? What do you consider to be a healthy fear?

_____

_____

_____

_____

_____

_____

4. Some say that we must fight fire with fire, others argue that fighting fire with fire results in an explosion and that we must instead fight fire with water. What is your opinion?

_____

_____

_____

_____

Additional Notes

September

Walk The Walk

Walk in the Spirit, and you shall not fulfill the lust of the flesh . . . If we live in the Spirit, let us also walk in the Spirit. Galatians 5:16, Galatians 5:25

The term "walk" is used dozens of times in the New Testament to describe the manner of life that a person is leading. Many of these occurrences depict the Christian life; for example, "walk in love . . . walk as children of light . . . walk circumspectly" (Ephesians 5:2, 8, 15). In this passage, we are told to "walk in the Spirit."

Walking is a very insightful description of spiritual life. A walk has a beginning and a destination. Our beginning was in new birth: "born of the Spirit." (John 3:6). Our destination is heaven forever with our Lord and Savior: "And thus we shall always be with the Lord." (1Thessalonians 4:17). A good walk is steady and progressive. We are called to be faithful: "Well done, good and faithful servant" (Matthew 25:21). We are called to press ahead: "forgetting those things which are behind and reaching forward to those things which are ahead, I press toward the goal" (Philippians 3:13-14).

In addition, a walk has many potential adventures along the way. We are likely to encounter stretching challenges and paradoxical blessings: "in tumults, in labors, in sleeplessness. . .

as sorrowful, yet always rejoicing; as poor, yet making many rich; as having nothing, and yet possessing all things" (2 Corinthians 6:5, 10).

Ultimately, a walk must have an available resource that provides sufficient vitality, strength, guidance, and assurance. Here, our passages offer special hope through the injunction to "walk in the Spirit." Day by day, each step of the way, we are to rely upon the presence and work of the Holy Spirit in our lives. Every issue of life (whether at home, office, school, or church) is to be faced in this manner. Otherwise, the influence of our flesh (our natural humanity) will prevail. "Walk in the Spirit, and you shall not fulfill the lust of the flesh." We are not able ourselves to overcome the inadequacies and improper tendencies of the flesh. However, the Holy Spirit is more than able to become our sufficient provider of whatever we need for an effective and fruitful walk.

This perspective on Christian living makes complete biblical sense, when we connect our daily walk to how we found spiritual life in the first place. "If we live in the Spirit, let us also walk in the Spirit," It was strictly by the work of the Spirit that we received life initially; therefore, let's take each step of life "[walking] in the Spirit."

There once was a man in a state medium security prison who wanted freedom. He came with a fool-proof plan to break out of prison. He was working in the laundry room and had the idea to hide himself in the laundry cart under the clothes as they were taken out of the prison in a truck. After a while someone pushed the laundry carts into a truck and drove for a while. Eventually the truck came to a stop and was parked. When the prisoner no longer heard anyone around he climbed out of the laundry cart and look up at the sign on the wall that read "Maximum Security Prison."

Do you ever struggle to gain freedom from besetting sins? Sins that you thought you should have conquered long ago? Maybe you recently did something that you knew was wrong but couldn't seem to resist the temptation. Maybe you have fasted about it and prayed about it but you end up falling into it. I think if we're honest we can all say that we struggle with sin in our lives and wonder how we can consistently live a life that pleases God. I realize that in this life we can never completely eradicate our sin nature but we can put it in subjection.

Above we looked at some other places in the scriptures where we are admonished to walk. There are three aspects to consider when attempting to "walk in the spirit." How do we do that? The answer does not come very simply.

We must recognize that we are triunal beings, made of three parts; body, soul and spirit.

a. The Body is that aspect of our personality that enables us to relate to the physical/material world. Most people define their identity or who they are based on this perspective. They describe themselves as: black or white, tall or short, fat or thin, etc. But this is not really you this is a part of you.

b. The Soul is the part of our personality that connects or relates both to the material world through the body and to the spiritual world through our spirit. It consist of your intellect/mind (which is your thought process unit), your will (which is your decision making unit) and your emotions (which is your expressive unit). People who view themselves from this perspective describe themselves with such phrases as: sensitive, stupid, intelligent, happy, forgetful, etc. Again this is just a part of you

c. The Spirit is the trickiest part of you. It is the part of you that enables you to relate to the Spirit world especially to God. It is the life of God in you. It is the image of God in you. Without the spirit, your body and soul will be dead. When we are born again it is in our spirit man, not in the soul or body.

The Holy Spirit is present to identify us, to help our spirit by empowering it, guiding it, revealing to it the will of God. Simply put - the *Holy Spirit* is there to train *our* spirit.

Romans 8:16 says, "The Spirit himself beareth witness with our spirit that we are the children of God." 2 Corinthians 1:22 (Amplified Bible): ... [He has also appropriated and acknowledged us as His by] putting His seal upon us and giving us His [Holy] Spirit in our hearts as the security deposit *and* guarantee [of the fulfillment of His promise]. Ephesians 1:13: In whom ye also trusted, after that ye heard the word of truth, the gospel of your salvation: in whom also after that ye believed, ye were sealed with that holy Spirit of promise,

So, "How can we walk in the Spirit?" We need to change our mindset. For a Christian it is a matter of our thought life. Satan's temptations and attacks are upon our thought life. Paul said the mind set on the flesh is death. The mind set on the Spirit is life and peace. Everything revolves around where we set our minds. There is a saying that if Satan can control our thought life he can control all our life.

Here are some additional scriptures to illustrate these thoughts further:

Prov. 23:7

Rom. 8:5

Colossians 3:1-3

Romans 12:2

Philippians 4:6-9

2 Corinthians 10:3-5

You might say, "I know all these scriptures but how do I apply it?" One word: Training. To overcome we must train our minds to think correctly. By reading the word, believing the word, meditating on the word and applying the word.

Hebrews 5:14: But solid food is for the mature, who by constant use have trained themselves to distinguish good from evil. What is good for you is to walk in the spirit. People don't get up and begin to walk when they are born. It is a process. Persistency is the key. We fall down but we get up.

How do I train my mind? The Word of God. This is the key to walking in the spirit. How do I know what is good? The Word of God.

Psalm 119:105 says: Your word is a lamp to my feet and a light for my path.

John 6:63: It is the spirit that quickeneth; the flesh profiteth nothing: the words that I speak unto you, they are spirit, and they are life.

Deut. 30:11-15: For this commandment which I command thee this day, it is not hidden from thee, neither is it far off. It is not in heaven, that thou shouldest say, Who shall go up for us to heaven, and bring it unto us, that we may hear it, and do it? Neither is it beyond the sea, that thou shouldest say, Who shall go over the sea for us, and bring it unto us, that we may hear it, and do it? But the word is very nigh unto thee, in thy mouth, and in thy heart, that thou mayest do it. See, I have set before thee this day life and good, and death and evil;

1 John 3:9: Whosoever is born of God doth not commit sin; for his seed remaineth in him: and he cannot sin, because he is born of God.

The fact is that you cannot continue to live in sin because the seed is in you. The seed is the word. 1 Peter 1:23: Being born again, not of corruptible seed, but of incorruptible, by the word of God, which liveth and abideth for ever.

Questions To Ask Myself This Month

1. Paul calls us to live by the Spirit and produce certain fruits. How many of these fruits have been evident in your actions and words over the last month?

_____

_____

_____

_____

2. How is the freedom of Christ, having crucified the sinful nature and living by the Spirit different from obeying the Law?

_____

_____

_____

_____

3. If you are led by the Spirit, how do you tell the difference between what you want and what the Spirit wants? Is there a difference?

_____

_____

_____

_____

4. Is there anything good in the flesh? Can you crucify our own desires and still remain the same person?

_____

_____

_____

_____

5. How can you keep renewing your commitment to walk by the Spirit? What specific steps can you take to make this a reality in your life? What role does your will and activity play in all of this process?

_____

_____

_____

Additional Notes

October

Supply And Demand

But my God shall supply all your need according to his riches in glory by Christ Jesus. Philippians 4:19

This verse is a popular verse often quoted out of context. "But my God shall supply all your need." The "but" indicates that verse 19 is an outcome of what has been previously said. This paragraph exhorts God's faithfulness in using the Philippians to meet the financial needs of Paul in jail. The Philippians met Paul's need. Now God will meet their need. This is a quid pro quo (one thing in return for another). God used the Philippians to meet Paul's need in jail. God will also meet the Philippians' ability to give. What affects Paul affects God. God will exchange compliments. God is faithful to his people. He will not stand in debt to his people.

The context of God meeting our financial needs is in the environment of our meeting the needs of others. In verse 18 the Philippians gave an acceptable sacrifice that was a sweet smelling aroma to God. If everything is flowing out and nothing flowing in, the Philippians will themselves be put in jeopardy financially. God will not allow those who give sacrificially to go in want. We cannot out give God. He has a bigger shovel. The promise here is that God will supply "all" the needs of the Philippians, not just some of them. God's supply is comprehensive of every type of need. Whether our need is temporal or spiritual, God will meet it.

"Give, and it shall be given unto you; good measure, pressed down, and shaken together, and running over, shall men give into your bosom. For with the same measure that ye mete withal it shall be measured to you again." (Luke 6:38).

"I have been young, and now am old; yet have I not seen the righteous forsaken, nor his seed begging bread." (Psalm 37:25).

"Honour the LORD with thy substance, and with the firstfruits of all thine increase: So shall thy barns be filled with plenty, and thy presses shall burst out with new wine." (Proverbs 3:9-10).

The Philippians not only were a help to a fellow man they were a blessing to Paul in his ministry. We can learn a lesson from them. The nature of true Christian sympathy is not only to feel concern for our leaders in their troubles, but to do what we can to help them. The apostle was often in bonds, imprisonments, and lacking necessities; but in all, he learned to be content, to bring his mind to his condition, and make the best of it. Pride, unbelief, and vain hankering after something we haven't got, make us discontented even under favorable circumstances. Let us pray for patient submission and hope when we are oppressed; for humility and a heavenly mind when exalted. It is a special grace to have an equal temper of mind, and when in a low state not to lose our comfort in God, nor distrust his provision, nor attempt to go ahead of Him.

The other hand is that in a prosperous condition we must not be proud, or secure, or worldly. This is a harder lesson than the other; for the temptations of fullness and prosperity are more than those of affliction and want. The apostle Paul had no design to urge them to give more, but to encourage such kindness as will meet a glorious reward hereafter. Through Christ we have grace to do what is good, and through him we must expect the reward; and as we have all things by him, let us do all things for him, and to his glory.

You may be thinking that as much as you'd like to be able to give into the ministry you are really in no financial position to do so. We are in tough economic times; this is a fact for all of us. Please do not feel unworthy if you don't have the resources of Donald Trump. This verse need not cause you to feel inadequate.

In the first place, the congregation of Jesus Christ in Philippi was anything but well off in financial terms. I say that because of what Paul writes to the Corinthians. There he writes about "the churches of Macedonia", and says that "in a great trial of affliction the abundance of their joy and their deep poverty abounded in the riches of their liberality." The only church of Macedonia mentioned anywhere in Scripture as generous in giving was the church in Philippi. Yet here they're described as experiencing "deep poverty". Here, then, is a particular need amongst the Philippians: despite their generosity, they're poor. Many people mistakenly believe that my husband and I are very well off financially. This is not true. We are not in want. We are not uncomfortable. But we certainly do not have an over abundance. What we do have – are giving hearts.

Are there other needs in Philippi? From the letter Paul wrote to the Philippians, it's clear that Paul himself is aware of others. I read, for example, in chapter 1:29 that the Philippians were suffering for Jesus' sake, indeed, they experienced the same conflict Paul was experiencing. That's a reference to persecution, to the hatred of the world (John 15:18; 2 Corinthians 11:24). In the face of hatred and persecution there was obviously need for courage, faithfulness and perseverance even in struggle.

Therefore the promise of verse 19 must instead be linked with verse 13, and both verses must be read in light of verses 11-12: God supplies the needs of his people by giving them the resources to cope with hardship. Hardship tempts us to think that God is unmoved by our plight or is against us, and so we despair. Thus, when we experience difficult times, we need the moderating presence of God, who shows us by the cross of Christ that he is for us, not against us.

The biggest need in the congregation, though, forms the meat of Paul's letter. You will recall: the congregation was divided and was afflicted with selfishness. Paul instructs the Philippians in chapter 1 to "stand fast in one Spirit, with one mind striving together for the faith of the gospel" (vs. 27), and that instruction implies that the Philippian saints –despite the care they showed to Paul over the years- were not standing side by side in the fight of faith. Chapter 2:3 says: "Let nothing be done through selfish ambition or conceit, but in lowliness of mind let each esteem the other better than himself."

Again, Paul says this because there was selfishness and conceit among the brethren (4:2), with each looking out for himself first of all. To straighten out that fault, the apostle gives the detailed and wonderful expose of how the Lord Jesus Christ gave up the glory of heaven in exchange for the shame of the cross in order to save the unworthy (2:5). Paul knows selfishness and its resulting friction are deadly for the church of Jesus Christ, and are essentially denials of what the church is all about. Nothing new under the sun is there? Yes, there was plenty of in the church of the Philippians!

Over the years the Philippians had given the apostle wonderful gifts, most recently through Epaphroditus. The culture of the day required that Paul express his gratitude by giving a gift in return. And yes, the Philippian saints had needs. But Paul, being in prison has no resources upon which to return his gratitude. The Philippians have a great financial need, but Paul in prison is powerless to give a material gift. The Philippians are persecuted on account of the faith, but Paul in prison is powerless to give relief from persecution. How, then, can Paul properly say thanks?

The answer is the words of our text: "my God shall supply all your need according to His riches in glory by Christ Jesus." From his prison cell Paul has nothing tangible to give in the face of the Philippians' needs. But Paul has something better to give the Philippians in their struggles, and that's the wealth of the gospel. That's how he expresses his gratitude: by giving more, much more the Philippians could ever give him. Paul has nothing inside to give them but he –apostle that he is- has something *outside of himself* to give to them, and that's the promise that *his God* will supply all their need. What a way to say Thank You!

Does Paul want the Philippians to think that God will supply their every need in this sense that He will deliver them from their financial distress, their persecutors, their selfishness? That question is so very important to us because we have tangible problems also, and if Paul's God will supply the Philippians in their real needs, surely we can be assured that God will supply us also in our real needs.

Notice then beloved, how the apostle speaks of God in our text. At the beginning of vs. 19 Paul describes God as 'my God'. Why that pronoun 'my'? What would be different if he had simply said 'God' or 'the Lord', or even 'our God'? Why 'my God'? Although it seems insignificant the question is important.

With that pronoun 'my', the apostle is drawing attention to the way God has supplied for Paul. As God has dealt with Paul, has supplied his every need, so God will deal with the Philippians – supply their every need.

How, then, has God supplied for the needs of the apostle? The book of Acts and the letters of Paul tell us a few things about what sort of life Paul was given to live. We already know that at the time he wrote this letter to the Philippians Paul was in prison. And this wasn't the first time; he'd been in and out of prison repeatedly. In fact, in 2 Corinthians 11:26 Paul relates the sort of things he suffered regularly. "From the Jews five times," Paul relates, "I received forty stripes minus one. Three times I was beaten with rods; once I was stoned; three times I was shipwrecked; a night and a day I have been in the deep; in journeys often, in perils of waters, in perils of robbers, in perils of my own countrymen, in perils of the Gentiles, in perils in the city, in perils in the wilderness, in perils in the sea, in perils among false brethren; in weariness and toil, in sleeplessness often, in hunger and thirst, in fastings often, in cold and nakedness" That was Paul's life: constantly hounded by efforts to silence God's emissary to the Gentiles. Had God supplied his needs?

Three times the apostle Paul had asked the Lord to take away these hellish attacks that hindered his preaching and increased his suffering, but the Lord God declined! (2 Corinthians 12:7). Instead, his life was characterized by difficulty, suffering, trials and tribulations! Is this the same apostle who writes that his God would supply the needs of the Philippians? What do you think beloved: how much encouragement is there in such a statement for these Philippians?! If the Lord will supply their need as He has supplied Paul's, their future certainly doesn't look bright at all! This is quite the conundrum. So we need to look more carefully at how the Lord has cared for Paul.

Here I draw your attention to the apostle's words in the verses before our text. He greatly appreciates - (verse 10) - that the Philippians have provided help for him again (now that they know where he is, in some prison cell). Paul appreciates it much, but (he adds in vs 11) it's not that I really have need. Sure, he says, I'm in prison and so I can't do what I want, and this stone prison is cold and damp, and there's rats around and it's smelly, and sometimes I'm hungry and I can't sleep because of the ravings of other prisoners. But, he says, "I have learned in whatever state I am, to be content." "I know," he says in verse 12, "I know how to be abased, and I know how to abound." I can be content with little, he says, and I can be content with much. Both are for Paul quite manageable.

So there's the question: why can Paul be so content in both good times and bad? What's his secret? He tells us in verse 13: "I can do all things through Christ who strengthens me." Paul is not a stronger person, a better Christian than everybody else so that he can boast of an inner reserve of strength that the

Philippians didn't have – and we don't either. Rather, Paul describes to the Philippians a work that daily takes place within him. What that work is? This: Christ strengthens him. That is to say: Jesus Christ gives Paul grace day by day not to get despondent in the face of adversity, not to get cynical in the face of injustice, not to get bitter in the face of wrong. For Paul "to live is Christ", and so he lays himself at Christ's disposal, willing to be of service in whatever manner Christ chooses.

Do you see why Paul begins this text with a reference to "my God"? God is the center of Paul's life, God is so very faithful – He uses Paul in His kingdom, and Paul considers that such a privilege that nothing else is important as long as he can serve. So you see, Christ supplies his needs so that he can serve! As Christ supplies the apostle's need, even in the valley of the shadow of death, so, says Paul, this God will supply every need the Philippians might have. Of that Paul has no doubt. He expresses his confidence that the Lord will supply the needs of the Philippians. Paul has experienced it himself, and he's sure that the God who supplies all his needs –gives grace to be content so that Paul knows who to be abased and how to abound- the God who supplies all his needs will supply the needs of the struggling saints of Philippi also. And of struggling saints all over the world.

What a promise! What an encouragement! But a question remains: is it really true that God will supply the Philippians in the way He has supplied for the apostle? On what grounds can we today be sure that the Lord will supply all our needs? That's my last point: the guarantee of Paul's statement. The guarantee lies in the concluding words of our text: "according to His riches in glory by Christ Jesus."

All the riches of all creation –from gold and silver on the one hand to power and peace on the other- belong to this God. This God who owns all dwells in eternal glory in heaven, with multitudes of angels who sing His praise and do His bidding. The phrase "riches in glory" describes the wealth of resources that God has at His disposal – resources so infinitely greater than Paul has at his disposal in the confines of his prison cell.

But God does not keep the resources at His disposal for Himself alone. He's rather pleased to share all this wealth and all this glory with His people. That's the force of the concluding words of our text: "by Christ Jesus." Christ Jesus is the *link* between this holy God and man on earth. Christ Jesus gave up His glory with the Father in order to redeem man to God. On the cross He paid for sin, reconciled sinners to God, so that sinners might be children of God once more. Now that these sinners are God's children again, the Lord in mercy gives of the abundance He has for the good of His people. That's the promise of God drawn out so often in Scripture, the promise whose truth the apostle has tasted himself in all the ups and downs of his life. From the abundance God has, God for Jesus' sake has supplied Paul's needs so that Paul could be content both in poverty and in riches, could be at peace in his heart even when storms were raging around him.

My husband, Dr. Robert E. Johnson has an often requested signature song that in his smooth baritone truly touches the spirit. The song is My Soul Has Been Anchored. I believe that the apostle Paul would have sung this very song. The song says:

> Though the storms keep on raging in my life;
> And sometimes it's hard to tell the night from day;
> Still that hope that lies within is reassured
> As I keep my eyes upon the distant shore;
> I know He'll lead me safely to that blessed place He has prepared.
>
> But if the storms don't cease,
> And if the winds keep on blowing in my life,
> My soul has been anchored in the Lord.

> (words and music by Douglass Miller)

Given those grounds for Paul's conviction that God will supply the needs of the Philippians, we may be assured too that the Lord supplies all our needs. No, not that He takes away all sickness today or all tension or all oppression; those things will be taken away on the day of Christ's return. Meanwhile, the God of all riches supplies for His own so that we can be at peace always.

So "Be anxious for nothing, but in everything by prayer and supplication, with thanksgiving, let your requests be made known to God; and the peace of God, which surpasses all understanding, will guard your hearts and minds through Christ Jesus" (4:6). Amen.

Questions To Ask Myself This Month

1. God will commemorate sacrificial giving. Are you generous with others? Are you a stingy person?

_____

_____

_____

_____

2. Do you tend to hang onto your money? Is it because you do not believe that God will supply your need? Do you believe that God will "resupply" you if you give to his cause?

_____

_____

_____

_____

3. God's commemorative giving does not apply to every believer. It only applies to those who have given sacrificially. When was the last time you gave beyond your immediate means? Did you get a 'return on your investment'? Was it financial?

_____

_____

_____

_____

4. This verse of scripture nor the lesson is an encouragement to give your money foolishly. We must use wisdom in our giving and make sure we also provide for ourselves. Do you have a savings account? Do you contribute to retirement plans, investments, or 401K plans? Do you have life insurance?

_____

_____

5. What other ways can you support your spiritual leaders and church homes besides financially?

_____

_____

_____

_____

Additional Notes

November

It Is Well With My Soul

God is our refuge and strength, a very present help in trouble.

Therefore will not we fear, though the earth be removed, and though

the mountains be carried into the midst of the sea;

Though the waters thereof roar and be troubled, though the

mountains shake with the swelling thereof. There is a river, the

streams whereof shall make glad the city of God, the holy place of

the tabernacles of the most High. God is in the midst of her; she

shall not be moved: God shall help her, and that right early. The

heathen raged, the kingdoms were moved: he uttered his voice, the

earth melted. The Lord of hosts is with us; the God of Jacob is our

refuge. Come, behold the works of the Lord, what desolations he

hath made in the earth. He maketh wars to cease unto the end of the

earth; he breaketh the bow, and cutteth the spear in sunder; he

burneth the chariot in the fire. Be still, and know that I am God: I will

be exalted among the heathen, I will be exalted in the earth. The

Lord of hosts is with us; the God of Jacob is our refuge. Selah.

Psalm 46:1-11

We all have days when we'd like to run away from it all. Sometimes our hurt is so bad our spirit throbs inside us.Our dreams fall apart, our hopes fade, our lives become wearisome drudgery, a marriage goes bad, health problems develop, financial problems come up, a loved one dies, and we are tempted to give up.

Though problems will still be a given, though difficulties will still touch us, though hardships will be a part of our lives, there is always a reason to keep going. We can press on! We can hang in there! We can go on when we want to give up.

Horatio G. Spafford, was born in North Troy, New York, on October 20, 1828. As a young lawyer Spafford established a very successful legal practice in Chicago. Despite his financial success, he always maintained a faithful interest in Christian activities. He enjoyed a close and active relationship with D. L. Moody, Phillip Bliss and other evangelical leaders of that era. Spafford was described as:"a man of unusual intelligence and refinement, deeply spiritual, and a devoted student of the Scriptures." Horatio Spafford had a close relationship with God.

Point #1: There is a divine presence.

God is our refuge and strength, a very present help in trouble.

· Notice the descriptive words in this verse:

· Refuge: it means "a shelter or hiding place."

· Strength:... "our security, boldness, might."

· Present: He is always with us.

· Help: this word means "aid or assist." He doesn't leave us to our own struggles alone.

· Trouble: it means "tight spots...misery, distress, agony, suffering, aggravation, ."

· In: this preposition means "not before or after but during, in the midst of".

· In all these problems...

God is our refuge, strength, and a present help.

The Bible says in Psalm 139: "Where can I go from Thy Spirit? Or where can I flee from Thy presence? If I ascend to heaven, Thou art there; If I make my bed in Sheol, behold, Thou art there. If I take the wings of the dawn, If I dwell in the remotest part of the sea, Even there Thy hand will lead me, And Thy right hand will lay hold of me.".

Jesus said: "...lo, I am with you always, even unto the end of the world." Matthew 28:20.

"If anyone loves Me, he will keep My word; and My Father will love him, and We will come to him, and make Our abode with him." John 14:23.

Horatio Spafford had a close relationship with God. But things started to happen to him when he was 43 years old. On October 9th of 1871, the Great Chicago Fire started. According to legend, a Mrs. O'Leary's cow kicked over a lantern in a barn to start the fire. 16 hours later, 3 and 1/2 square miles of Chicago were burned to the ground. Spafford's holdings were wiped out by this disaster. The Spaffords had a consistent history of acting on their faith. After the Chicago fire, they devoted countless hours to helping the survivors.

In November of 1873, Horatio Spafford planned a trip to Europe to hear Moody preaching his revivals. As winter began to chill their Chicago home, Horatio, his wife Anna, and their four young daughters, 11 year old Annie, 9 year old Maggie, 7 year old Bessie, and 2 year old Tanetta, began to anticipate the sea voyage. When the time for the trip drew close, Spafford's business encountered some difficulties that required him to remain at home. Determined not to deprive his family of the anticipated trip, he kissed his wife and daughters good-bye, and promised to join them as soon as possible.

The Spafford women boarded the French steamer, Ville de havre, and began their trans-Atlantic journey. Off the coast of Newfoundland, however, tragedy struck. On November 22, The ship collided with an English ship, the Loch Earn, ripping a gaping hole in the ship's hull. The Ville de Havre plunged to the bottom of the frigid sea within 12 minutes. In the moments before the ship sank, Anna Spafford gathered her 4 young girls to her side and prayed with them, holding the youngest –Tanetta - in her arms. As the icy waters of the North Atlantic swept over the decks, the 3 older children disappeared. Eventually even the baby was washed from her mother's arms.

Anna was able to cling to a piece of floating wreckage. Alone and near death herself, Anna was spotted from a lifeboat and plucked from the sea. She was among the 61 passengers and 26 crew members who survived. Two hundred and twenty six lost their lives. It was 10 days before the survivors of the shipwreck landed safely in Cardiff, Wales. From there Anna Spafford sent a telegram to her anxious husband It was a brief and distressing message: "Saved alone. What Shall I Do?"

Boarding the next available ship out of New York, Horatio sailed to Cardiff, Wales, where he was reunited with his grieving wife. In the mid-Atlantic ocean, the ship's captain called Spafford to the bridge and said, "To the best of my calculations, Mr. Spafford, this is where the tragedy occurred and your four little daughters were drowned." Horatio G. Spafford stood on the bridge contemplating the loss of his girls. He stayed there for some time and then went to his cabin and wrote the poem that begins *"When peace like a river attendeth my way."*

What depth of pain-filled grief must have flooded over him. The Holy Spirit inspired him to pen these words, *"When sorrows like sea billows roll; Whatever my lot, Thou has taught me to say, it is well, it is well, with my soul."* The Spafford's close friend, evangelist Dwight L. Moody, was in Edinburgh, Scotland, at the time of the tragedy and came from there to join the grieving couple. He later reported of that meeting that, though they were experiencing deep sorrow, the Spaffords never lost their abiding faith in God.

Friends can be a comfort and encouragement during difficult circumstances. This grieving, loving father longed for the day when he would see his 4 beautiful daughters again. *"And Lord haste the day when the faith will be sight, the clouds be rolled back as a scroll; the trump shall resound and the Lord shall descend, even so, it is well with my soul."*

The hope of being reunited with their beloved children gave these parents the courage to keep on living in faith. Their hearts were comforted and strengthened by the truth of the resurrection.

Point #2: There is a divine promise.

Therefore will not we fear, though the earth be removed, and though the mountains be carried into the midst of the sea; Though the waters thereof roar and be troubled, though the mountains shake with the swelling thereof. There is a river, the streams whereof shall make glad the city of God, the holy place of the tabernacles of the most High. God is in the midst of her; she shall not be moved: God shall help her, and that right early.

"God will help us." We may go through a long night of sorrow and suffering but the dawn brings God's help. Psalm 30:5 says: weeping may endure for a night, but joy cometh in the morning. What do we do in the face of troubles? Some forget God's promises and go it alone. They face temptation alone and fall into sin, bound then to live with guilt and failure. They get into a tight place alone and find themselves outmatched, outnumbered and outwitted by the difficulties of life.

They try to handle the problems of life alone and become afraid. Some doubt God's promises and act as if there is no real hope. They worry and fret and fuss. Romans 3:4 says: "Let God be found true, though every man be found a liar." 2 Timothy 1:12 :…Whoever else you may not believe…believe God. nevertheless I am not ashamed: for I know whom I have believed, and am persuaded that he is able to keep that which I

116

have committed unto him against that day." Believe Jesus when He said, "I am the resurrection and the life; he who believes in Me shall live even if he dies," John 11:25. That unshakable confidence provided a reason to go on in faith.

Returning to Chicago, Spafford rejoined his legal practice. Once again, he became active in the local Presbyterian church as an elder and working with the YMCA. A visitor to his office 2 years after the shipwreck asked about the telegram in a frame above Spafford's desk carrying only the words, "Saved alone." Spafford told the man the full story and again affirmed, "It is well. God's will be done." The Spaffords had 2 more daughters and 1 son born after the tragedy. But sorrow and tragedy would strike them again.

In 1880, their 4-year-old son, Horatio, came down with scarlet fever. In spite of the efforts by the best physicians in Chicago, Spafford's son died. Some members of the Presbyterian congregation to which the Spaffords belonged believed that some sin in their lives had caused all these tragedies. They kept telling the Spaffords to repent. (Anyone else see the resemblance to Job?) But Spafford said: *"It Is Well With My Soul"*

Point #3: There is a divine peace

Therefore will not we fear, though the earth be removed, and though the mountains be carried into the midst of the sea; Be still, and know that I am God: I will be exalted among the heathen, I will be exalted in the earth.

"Relax" or "Be still." Stop fighting it so hard! Quit struggling against it. How can we do that? "Know that I am God." Remember that God is God, that God reigns, that God is still on his Throne. Then, and only then, can we say "Therefore will not we fear, though the earth be removed, and though the mountains be carried into the midst of the sea…"

· This means believing that God is all powerful, all knowing, and all present.

· This means bringing our stresses and fears to Him and seeking His help.

· This means trusting God with all our problems.

· This means resting in Him as our refuge.

Jesus knew our tendency to fear and be restless; He spoke these powerful words: John 14:1 "Let not your heart be troubled; believe in God, believe also in Me." John 14:27 "Peace I leave with you, my peace I give unto you: not as the world giveth, give I unto you. Let not your heart be troubled, neither let it be afraid."

The opposition grew until finally the Spaffords were asked to leave their church. And with unwavering faith and trust in God, they departed. Long interested in biblical archaeology, Spafford decided to leave the United States. In 1881, at the age of 53, he and his wife and 2 daughters moved to Jerusalem. There they founded an American colony where they spent the rest of their lives.

The words "it is well with my soul" are not found in scripture, But Jesus did say, "Come to me, all ye that labour and are heavy laden…and ye shall find rest unto your souls" (Matthew 11:28-29).

Our compassionate heavenly Father gives us comfort, hope and peace in his Son Jesus Christ. I found refuge in this peace when I lost my beloved father; Apostle Monroe R. Saunders Sr. My father was and is such a large part of me and in losing him I lost a part of me. His spirit lingers with me every minute of every day but I still miss him. Every now and then I still shed a tear for my daddy. One day God will wipe away every tear and there will be no more death or mourning or crying or pain. Horatio Spafford died in the faith of malaria in 1888. His daughter, Bertha Spafford Vester, led the group to establish the

American Colony Hotel, which has provided a welcome oasis for travelers to Jerusalem for more than a century. What a fitting tribute to the one who gave us these words to sing:

When peace, like a river, attendeth my way,
When sorrows like sea billows roll;
Whatever my lot, Thou has taught me to say,
It is well, it is well, with my soul.

Refrain
It is well, with my soul,
It is well, with my soul,
It is well, it is well, with my soul.

Though Satan should buffet, though trials should come,
Let this blessed assurance control,
That Christ has regarded my helpless estate,
And hath shed His own blood for my soul.
Refrain

My sin, oh, the bliss of this glorious thought!
My sin, not in part but the whole,
Is nailed to the cross, and I bear it no more,
Praise the Lord, praise the Lord, O my soul!
Refrain

And Lord, haste the day when my faith shall be sight,

The clouds be rolled back as a scroll;

The trump shall resound, and the Lord shall descend,

Even so, it is well with my soul.

Questions To Ask Myself This Month

1. Have you ever gone through a Job or Horatio period in your life? A time when you felt as if you had lost everything that meant anything to you? How did it affect your faith in God?

_____

_____

_____

_____

2. Is there a particular song or poem that touches a place deep in your spirit when you are going through?

_____

_____

_____

_____

3. Maybe you are not much of a writer but can you write at least a few lines that can detail and heal a situation in your life? It need not rhyme and need not be long and no one ever has to see it but you.

_____

_____

_____

_____

_____

4. Oftentimes the people who are closest to us are the ones who hurt us the most. This is when we need to lean on the Lord more than ever. (Psalm 146:3-6) Have you ever had to choose between your friends and your faith?

_____

_____

_____

5. When we get into trouble usually we work hard to get ourselves out of it. Letting go and letting God is not always easy. The next time you find yourself in a jam and trying to fix it how can you "be still"?

_____

_____

Additional Notes

December

The Good, The Bad, And The Ugly

And we know that all things work together for good to them that love God, to them who are the called according to his purpose. Romans 8:28

Mark Smith, in an article in Readers Digest said the following: Like many high school seniors, my son was filling out college scholarship applications. One form asked for extracurricular activities. He answered: "wrestling." The next question requested positions held. He entered: "pinned, mostly." --Mark Smith, Readers Digest June 2000 (http://www.irsweb.com/)

How many of you have felt like you are continually being "pinned" to the mat and are just waiting to get counted out. Maybe you have been hit with so much adversity you feel like the little girl who was riding along on her bike when she bumped her head on the low hanging branch of a tree. She ran into the house hollering, "Mom! Mom, Joey hurt me!" Mom looked up from what she was doing and said, "Sissy, Joey didn't hurt you. Joey's not even here. He went to the grocery store with your daddy." The little girl got this startled look on her face. Then in a bewildered sort of voice she said, "That means stuff like this can happen on its own at anytime. Whoa, bummer!"

In the issue of discouragement, one of the great things we can enjoy in Christ is freedom from that discouragement. Many times in this devotional we have seen reasons why we can have freedom from discouragement. One reason is that we know that better things are coming, There is more to this life. Secondly we can be free from discouragement because of the ministry and work of the Holy Spirit in our lives.

In this chapter Paul reminds us that our God is bigger than our problems. His plans are bigger than our problems. When we are suffering through difficult times, we can know that God will cause the bad situation to work together for good. This verse of Romans uses the word "know" to remind us that we can know God causes all things to work together for good. The word "know" means to learn by instruction. How do we know our math facts? By instruction. We know that God causes all things to work together for good because we are taught through God's word this is true. The only way we know this fact is through the teaching of the Bible.

If it were not for the revelation of the Word we would tend to think that too many things that happen in life work for evil instead of God. How many times have you seen what seemed like a hopeless situation turn into something good? I have seen some of the most difficult situations in life turn into something good for people. In my own life there have been many things that happened that at the time did not seem good, but later I could see they were the best thing that happened to me or they led to something really good.

Joseph M. Stowell (president of Cornerstone University and author of over 20 books) tells a story about his childhood. "Growing up in Hackensack, N.J., just across the George Washington Bridge from New York City, provided a variety of experiences for me. One was going to school with some of the rough kids from the neighboring town of South Hackensack. I recall one afternoon, playfully sparring with one of the Southside guys and having his punch actually land on my face. The blow jarred one of my front teeth loose. Thankfully, the dentist was able to anchor the tooth again, and I didn't lose it. In fact, I was better off--the tooth had always been crooked, so the dentist straightened it as he worked. Sometimes the blows of life have a way of taking something crooked and making it straight."

We are told that God causes *ALL THINGS* to work together for good. In the context of the book thus far, all things includes all the trials and tribulations we deal with in life. It deals with the persecutions we face as a result of our faith. We have some examples in the scriptures of this principle. How many of you think it would be terrible to be sold into slavery by your own brothers? Then how many of you think it would be bad to be thrown into prison for something you were completely innocent of after things seemed to be going well for you? This all happened to a man named Joseph. Later on in his life, Joseph's brothers thought Joseph was going to get them back when Joseph said the following in Genesis 50:20, "But as for you, you meant evil against me; *but* God meant it for good, in order to bring it about as *it is* this day, to save many people alive. (NKJV)

When the early church was being persecuted, it seemed like a bad thing, but the good out of it was the fact it made the Christians leave Jerusalem and take the gospel to other parts of the world. Acts 8:4 tells, "But the believers who had fled Jerusalem went everywhere preaching the Good News about Jesus." Whatever we are facing in life, God promises that it will work together for good. Who is that promise for? Is it for every person or just a limited few? Look at the rest of verse 28. This promise is for those who love God and who are called according to His purpose.

The passage implies that those who continually love God are the ones for whom this promise is for. We have learned in Romans 6:13 that if we love God, we will present ourselves to Him. In 6:22 we learn that if we love God, we will grow in sanctification (or we will become more holy and Christ-like in our lives). In chapter eight, we have learned that if we love God, we will walk according to the Spirit. John 14:21 (GWT) Whoever knows and obeys my commandments is the person who loves me. Those who love me will have my Father's love, and I, too, will love them and show myself to them."

The promise is for those who are called according to God's purpose. The word "purpose" means to place something before one's mind, to plan, to resolve. This verse then implies that a 'called' one is one who has heard the call and has accepted it and obeyed it. We are called through the gospel to God. Romans 10:17 says: "So then faith cometh by hearing, and hearing by the word of God. Romans 1:16 says: "For I am not ashamed of the gospel of Christ: for it is the power of God unto salvation to every one that believeth; to the Jew first, and also to the Greek." Now let us look at the purpose God had in making His plan. This purpose will help us to understand why God works through our difficult times.

One of the purposes behind God's plan was to see those who love Him be conformed to the image of Jesus. The word we translate "conformed" is a word that means a likeness inside and out. A thorough change, not just an outward superficial resemblance. One of the purposes for God working in our lives through the difficult times is so that one day we will have the same resurrection body that Jesus has. We will look like Him. In the mean time we are to allow ourselves to be transformed into His image.2 Corinthians 3:18 (NLT): "And all of us have had that veil removed so that we can be mirrors that brightly reflect the glory of the Lord. And as the Spirit of the Lord works within us, we become more and more like him and reflect his glory even more."

Romans 12:2: "And be not conformed to this world: but be ye transformed by the renewing of your mind, that ye may prove what is that good, and acceptable, and perfect, will of God." This is the destiny for those who love God. God does not want us to fail to reach this goal for our lives because it is part of a bigger plan for us. The second purpose behind God's plan was for Him to have a large family!

In verse 29 we are told that God wants Jesus to be the firstborn of many brethren. What this means is that God wants a big family. Jesus was resurrected and given a new body and now is seated at the right hand of the Father. He wants many others to follow the path of Jesus. Remember, the reason we are given freewill is because God only wants those in His family because they love Him. Giving us freewill is the only way for God to know we love Him. I wonder if Bill Gates came out and said he would adopt ANYONE who loved him into his family, how many people would say they loved him. How would he know if people really loved him? When you have great wealth that would be one of the perils of wealth, knowing who really loves you for you or who loves what you have. Don't you want people to love you for who you are? God is no different.

Let's look briefly at the process behind God's plan.

1. Foreknowledge: Verse 29 talks about those whom God foreknew. In the context the word "foreknew" means to "approve

of beforehand." What this means is that in eternity past, God knew He would approve of anyone who accepted His Son. He foreknew that those who accepted Jesus would be accepted by Him. God approves those who are faithful.

2. Predestine: The passage says He predestined them to be conformed to His image. Once again, this deals with the fact that God decided beforehand that those who accept Jesus would be conformed to His image, that we would have a resurrection body.

3. Called: He says that those whom He predestined, He also called. The ones who are predestined to glory are those who accept the call of the gospel. The call is open to everyone. 2 Timothy 2:4 tells us that God desires *all* to be saved and come to a knowledge of the truth. Those who reject the call are lost, those who accept are saved.

4. Justified: The one's called are justified. Remember that being justified means that we are declared innocent. If you are guilty, you cannot go to heaven, we can declare ourselves innocent, God is the only one who can do that, and that is done to those who answer the call of Jesus.

5. Glorified: When it is all said and done, when Jesus returns, we will be glorified with Jesus. We will be a brother or sister of Jesus. We will receive our inheritance in full from God

The purpose God has behind His plan and the process behind the plan are some of the reasons that God works through our trials and problems to make them work out for good. God does not want us to fail or to think that Satan is more powerful than He is. Pain and suffering are a reality of this world, as long as we live this life; it will be a part of life. All that will pass when we go to heaven.

Great minds have purposes, others have wishes. Little minds are tamed and subdued by misfortune; but great minds rise above them. --Washington Irving (Writer of The Legend of Sleepy Hollow and Rip Van Winkle)

We have a great God who will help us rise above the misfortunes in life! Don't be discouraged; look for the silver lining in the cloud of distress. Through all the tests, trials, storms, and pain – it will work out for your good. God loves you. You are His seed and He has a purpose for you!

Questions To Ask Myself This Month

1. Have you ever considered that pain has a purpose? Pain is nature's way of alerting us that something is wrong. For women it may be a sign that they are ready to deliver. When has pain in your life led to deliverance?

_____

_____

_____

_____

2. Do you think you have found God's purpose for your life? What is it? Are you still searching? What might you do to find it? (Ephesians 4:1-12)

_____

_____

_____

_____

3. We discussed how we learn by instruction. Learning and understanding the Word of God is imperative in the life of the believer. Construct a plan to add more Bible study time into your daily routine.

_____

_____

_____

_____

4. Think of an event in your life when, at the time, you thought it was the worst possible thing that could happen but as time went on you realized that event turned out for your good.

_____

_____

_____

_____

_____

Additional Notes

References

Barclay's Daily Study Bible

Gill's Exposition of the Entire Bible

David Rig Gospel Chapel
#1 Church Street
Bone Gap, Illinois

Sermon Central

Bible Gateway.com

Bible Hub.com

http://www.irsweb.com/

Grace Point Devotions

Journey of a Lifetime by Tommy Higle

Jacqueline Faye Saunders-Johnson, the

eldest daughter to the late Chief Apostle, Dr. Monroe R.
Saunders Sr. and Mother Alberta B. Saunders - founders of the
United Church of Jesus Christ, Apostolic, comes from a religious
family having been born the second in line of six children (3
sisters and 2 brothers).

She is the product of the Baltimore City Public School
System having graduated with honors from Forest Park Senior
High School and from Morgan State University with a Bachelor
of Science Degree in Music Education. Pastor Jackie (as she is
affectionately called) has pursued graduate coursework from the
College of Notre Dame, Baltimore, MD; Loyola University
Pastoral Care Program, Columbia, MD; and the Masters
International School of Divinity, Indiana.

Pastor Jackie married Bishop Robert E. Johnson, Sr. on
December 27, 1969 and from this union has come 3 wonderful

children: Keturah Desiree, Katherine Faye, and Robert Johnson, Jr., Esquire(Leslie). She is the proud grandmother of 5 wonderful grandchildren: Nicholas, Robert Monroe, Kennedy, Amaya, and Kamryn.

In the secular world, Pastor Jackie has taught for a number of years in the Baltimore City Public School System as a music teacher. She ended her teaching career by retiring from the St. Mark Catholic School in Catonsville, MD in June, 2012, after serving as the vocal music teacher and the choir director for 14 years.

In the church, Pastor Jackie has served as the National Minister of Music for the United Church for many years. She has given concerts across this country, Europe, Canada, and Jamaica. It was in 1977 that she first heard the call to expand her ministry beyond the musical scales. In 1985, she was consecrated as an evangelist and in 1996, she was elevated to be an ordained Elder and became the co-pastor with her husband of the New Jerusalem Praise Tabernacle (formerly known as New Jerusalem Deliverance Temple) where The Power is in the Love and the Deliverance is in your Praise. Upon the recommendation of her husband, Bishop Robert E. Johnson, Sr., Pastor Jackie was consecrated and installed as the Pastor of New Jerusalem Praise Tabernacle in July, 2002.

This anointed woman of God is chosen and sent by God to be a weapon against satan. She is a woman full of the Holy Ghost and Power that the Lord is using in these last days. She has the gift of laying on of hands and is known for her deliverance ministry and work at the altar. She is well qualified to preach and teach the Word of God, for she has a praying spirit and will yield herself to the Lord. She has been a blessing to the United Church worldwide, her family, her local church, community, and the body of Christ.

Her foremost prayer is found in the words of the song: "Jesus use me, and Oh Lord don't refuse me.- For surely there's a work that I must do. And even though it's humble, Lord help my will to crumble - And though the cost be great I'll work for you.

"The Power Is In The Love!"

Other Titles Available From Elohim Multimedia

Whose Blood Did Christ Shed?
An In-depth Look at the Bloodline of Jesus and its Effects on the Modern Day Body of Christ
By Briana C. CaBell

Chasing Shadows:
Revelations of a Young Mind
By Briana C. CaBell

Dream Catcher:
Tales of Love and Life, lost and found
By Briana C. CaBell

More titles coming soon...